Life in a
Teenage
Jungle

LIFE IN A TEENAGE JUNGLE

WILLIAM COLEMAN

Fleming H. Revell
A Division of Baker Book House Co
Grand Rapids, Michigan 49516

Published by Fleming H. Revell
a division of Baker Book House Company
P.O. Box 6287, Grand Rapids, MI 49516-6287

Printed in the United States of America

Library of Congress Cataloging-in-Publication Data

Coleman, William L.
  Life in a teenage jungle/ William Coleman.
      p.   cm.
  ISBN 0-8007-5525-1
  1. Teenagers—Prayer-books and devotions—English. 2. Teenagers—
Religious life. {1. Prayer books and devotions. 2. Conducts of life.} I. Title.
  BV4850. C5654 1994
  242' .63—dc20   94-5741

Contents

Contents

The transmitter is open.

Something as complex as a satellite to Mars becomes useless if it loses its communication system. Then this sophisticated piece of equipment has no way of either sending or receiving vital information.

Fortunately for us, our transmitter to God remains open. Daily we are able to send and receive signals from our heavenly Father. Smart people keep in touch.

A Lion in the Streets and Other Thoughts

Painted Smiles

Every Halloween, groups in our town offer to paint faces on trick-or-treaters. Some charge a buck or two; others do it for free. Instead of wearing bulky masks that might reduce vision, the children wear actors' makeup.

The new face doesn't tell us much about the person. For instance, an innocent nine-year-old may have the fiendish look of a werewolf. A shy, quiet child may look like a clown. The artist may paint a huge red smile on a person who is really sad and discouraged inside.

Our looks don't always tell the story of how we actually feel. How many times have you gone to school feeling like a hairball on the inside, while forcing yourself to be pleasant and calm as an airline flight attendant on the outside?

None of us feels happy all the time. Even Jesus got discouraged and hungry and upset. There isn't anything wrong with a few down times. But for some of us the down times come too often. Most of our smiles are pretend. We use them to cover up anguish inside.

If you want to smile more often without painting it on, try these two suggestions. They aren't the only ways to be happy, but they are a good start.

First, decide that you will be cheerful. All of us have problems, and some folks grump day and night. But there are many people who choose to be happy despite their headaches, lack of money, or anything else.

Second, keep in close contact with God. Our communication with God helps us see the brighter side of life. God is big on encouragement, optimism, dreams, hope, and pizza. He isn't the God of

10

gloom and grimness. Walks and talks with God can change our attitudes and make our faces open up like large cinnamon rolls.

A happy heart makes the face cheerful, but heartache crushes the spirit.

Proverbs 15:13

Think It Over

1. Name three things you could smile about.
2. Picture God smiling.
3. When do you find yourself talking to God?

A Lion in the Streets

Kristi always wanted to try new things. She wanted to water ski, go out for the basketball team, and apply for a scholarship to Spain. There was no end to the list of places she wanted to go and the things she wanted to do. Her days and nights were made up of dreams, hopes, and ambitions. The only problem was that Kristi never got further than wishing. When it came time to try out, apply, or get on the bus, Kristi always backed out and gave up.

She had the will, but she remained a wanna-be. Inside this talented and capable teenager lived crippling fears. Kristi was afraid. And when she didn't know what she was afraid of, she simply made up excuses.

In her mind the players on the basketball team were taller or faster than she. Waterskiing was too rough because it would get water up her nose. And when it came to scholarships, she figured they probably went to rich girls at private schools.

Kristi was as good at making excuses as she was at dreaming. In fact, she was better. For every ambition she seemed to have 203 excuses.

Fear has a way of making losers out of us all. Most of us have piles of unfulfilled dreams—things we never tried. Good, exciting, worthwhile, helpful, God-serving goals that would have been terrific to accomplish. But instead we make up excuses and never carry through.

The Bible tells us that some people are simply lazy. They talk good dreams, but they never make them come true. When it comes time to turn them into reality, they say, "Oh, I better not go. There might be a lion in the street and it will attack me." Or

12

else they are afraid that someone taller, faster, or smarter will beat them to it.

What is the dream you want to carry out this week? Would you rather go after it or make up excuses?

The sluggard says, "There is a lion in the road, a fierce lion roaming the streets!"

Proverbs 26:13

Think It Over

1. What activity would you like to try in school? Why don't you?
2. What group would you like to join at church? Why don't you?
3. What are some of your favorite excuses?

Family Turmoil

Every day Brad wondered what his family would be like that evening. He had learned to picture his home life much like a jungle. Some evenings were quiet with just a little chirping in the background. Weekends reminded him of roaring lions and rhinoceroses charging through the forest.

Brad never knew what might happen next. His father could be friendly one day and a howling monkey the next. His mother would be calm like an alligator along the shore; but if you got close to her, she could attack and snap at you.

His parents were doing battle, and he was certain their marriage wouldn't last. It hurt Brad to see and feel so much pain. He thought it was unfair that his world had turned into a jungle. His grades were dropping, and he had lost interest in most things.

Brad is typical of millions of teenagers who have seen their families in turmoil. Events are unpredictable. Parental moods swing without warning, and the young person doesn't know when he or she is safe.

The Psalm writer must have had all kinds of people in mind when he wrote about God and a place of safety. Certainly confused, bewildered teenagers in jungle-like homes are in need of a safe place where they can find peace.

God doesn't promise to take the jungle away. Neither does he promise to quiet the roaring beasts. But our heavenly Father offers us a sense of peace and security in the middle of all the racket.

This must be why so many teenagers turn to Jesus Christ. In a crazy world of surprises we need someone we can depend on. We come to Christ because he never changes and never moves away.

Peace comes from knowing that God does not leave us or forsake us. He loves us even when everything around us is out of control in every direction.

> I will lie down and sleep in peace, for you alone, O LORD, make me dwell in safety.
>
> *Psalm 4:8*

Think It Over

1. Would you describe your home life as a park, a forest, a city, or a jungle? Why?
2. When your family gets hectic, where do you find peace?
3. Do you ever discuss your home situation with God? How does that make you feel?

MTV Watching

What will happen if you watch too many music videos? Will your brains rot? Will you start to drool in public? Will you climb trees or howl like wolves?

Probably none of these things will happen, but that doesn't mean there is no danger. MTV and other music video shows could have a damaging effect.

Some of the videos are terrific with good sound, great visuals, and a first-class message. Videos are part of a youth culture that on the one hand is powerful and positive, but on the other hand walks along the edge and occasionally falls into the pits.

If you are going to watch stations like MTV, you would be smart to keep several things in perspective.

1. Establish personal morals based on the Bible and not according to a rock star.
2. Don't start to look at people as objects, especially as sex objects.
3. Don't overdose on music videos or on anything else. Be well-rounded.
4. If your parents tell you to turn off a video, turn it off.

Music is a lot of fun, but it isn't everything. Certainly young people should be able to define their own tastes and style. But anyone who hands his mind and morals over to a rock group or program has entered the goofy zone.

Loose sex, alcohol, and drug abuse may sound appealing when an exciting rock star promotes them, but don't be fooled. Young people are being led astray, and too many wake up sorry.

God doesn't want to see anyone hurt. He doesn't want to see you injure yourself or others. That's why God calls us away from immorality and toward himself.

With persuasive words she led him astray; she seduced him with her smooth talk.

Proverbs 7:21

Think It Over

1. What effect do music videos have on you?
2. Are there any videos you would take off the air?
3. Do you think videos pull you away from God? Explain.

Tightfisted

If you know of a family that has fallen into rough financial times, how are you likely to respond to their needs? Would you:

Give them your old eight-track tapes?
Lecture them about thriftiness?
Remind them that the poor are blessed?
Volunteer to walk their dog?
Contribute some of your own money?

When you heard about people losing their property during the floods in mid-America in 1993, how did you respond?

You tried not to watch the evening news.
You drank less water.
You sent food and clothing.
You volunteered to fill sandbags.
You sent your old rubber boots.
You prayed for the rain to stop.

When you hear that a home has burned down, you respond to the family's needs by:

Offering to buy their scorched television set.
Sending them used tea bags.
Taking the children into your home.
Calling them on the phone and singing cheery music.
Taking them bags of groceries.
Offering to feed their cat.
Giving some of your clothing.

18

From the early days in the history of Israel, God taught his people to be generous and to help others. He told us to open our clenched fists and give to those who are in need.

Often teenagers give very freely to others, especially if they see a child or another young person suffering. God encourages us to open up and continue to help others.

If there is a poor man among your brothers in any of the towns of the land that the LORD your God is giving you, do not be hardhearted or tightfisted toward your poor brother.

Deuteronomy 15:7

Think It Over

1. When did you last help someone in financial stress?
2. What kind of person are you most likely to help?
3. Why did God teach us to help others?

Angry and Armed

When we get red-hot angry, most of us want to punch something. We pound on the furniture, slam doors, kick at the cat. Pillows take a terrible beating from time to time. These are normal, even healthy, outlets for most of us.

Unfortunately thousands of frustrated teenagers have stopped hitting basketballs and walls and have now turned to serious violence. Last year the number of young teenagers (13 to 16) who were arrested for murder rose dramatically. The FBI reported over 1,500 homicide arrests in this age group. Most of these were males. If you go to a school where weapons are commonplace, this is probably no big surprise. You've seen hostility and violence.

There is no easy solution to deep-rooted problems, but a couple of things would certainly help. First, we need to cut back on our anger and frustration. Second, we need to find better ways to express our hostility. Young people who fight over concert tickets can't be allowed to run home and get a pistol.

It's okay to get angry sometimes. Some terrible situations do exist that should make us upset. But our anger has to be controlled. We can't go around pushing people off buildings or setting fire to cars.

Anger also has to have a short life span. Anger that lasts for days and weeks grows so large that we have trouble handling it. We need to express our anger and then let it die. Anger that builds up over a period of time can make the best of us turn to violence.

Let's ask God to help us soothe our hostilities. Few things are worth getting angry over, and none are worth violence. God can help us see what is really important and calm us down.

Anger is cruel and fury overwhelming.
Proverbs 27:4

Think It Over

1. Do you have a short fuse and get angry quickly?
2. How do you express your anger?
3. Can you think of a better way to express it?

Call Waiting

Imagine you come home after school and hear the answering machine beeping. Why not push the button? Maybe you've won the lottery or Hollywood saw your picture and wants you in its next action adventure. What if it's the president and he wants you to head up a national youth council?

And then again it could be some dweeb wanting to borrow your social studies notes.

But if you thought . . . what if you had reason to believe . . . what if you were very suspicious . . . that God had left a call on the machine? That God put a message on your phone, and he wanted you to call him back? How anxious would you be to punch the button and take the call?

Have you ever felt that God was telling you something? Did you ever feel a burden, a conviction, a force, a compelling need to do something, and that conviction wouldn't go away? I have.

If you thought that God wanted you to do something, would you punch the button, listen to the message, and carry it out?

Before you answer too quickly, read Jonah 1:1–3. God gave Jonah a call, and Jonah heard the message. Then Jonah hung up the phone and ran away. He didn't want to do what God told him to do. Instead he headed for the high seas and sailed away from God.

It's hard to say how often God leaves a message on your machine. Once a week, once a month, once a year. Who's to say? But we need to punch the button, listen to the call, and carry it out. That's what children of God are supposed to do.

But Jonah ran away from the LORD and headed for Tarshish. He went down to Joppa, where he found a ship bound for that port. After paying the fare, he went aboard and sailed for Tarshish to flee from the LORD.

Jonah 1:3

Think It Over

1. Would you like to hear a message from God?
2. Have you ever felt that God wanted you to do something?
3. Did you do it?

Top Ten Lies

There are groups, individuals, and even forces in our world that are spreading lies. They tell lies because they are selfish, uninformed, greedy, mean, or evil. The following may be ten of the biggest lies going around. They are not arranged in any order of importance. See if you can add to this list.

1. Come on, nobody ever gets caught.
2. You can't get addicted to this stuff.
3. Everybody does it.
4. If you get in trouble, I'll help you.
5. Only idiots get pregnant.
6. A few drinks never hurt anyone.
7. If you really loved me, you'd do it.
8. I'll give you back twice that much.
9. You can't get a disease this way.
10. Nobody believes that anymore.

Often we believe lies because we want to. We want to do something wrong, dumb, foolish, or evil, and we're ready to accept any phony explanation.

If we live on the edge, eager to do something stupid, we are easy targets for both little lies and big ones. For every person who is willing to believe a lie, there must be a dozen people ready to tell them one.

Speaking of the devil, Jesus said: "When he lies, he speaks his native language, for he is a liar and the father of lies."

John 8:44

Think It Over

1. What lie would you add to the list?
2. What lie have you fallen for?
3. Have you ever lied to get someone to do something?

The Great Date Escape

Jenny was nervous. She barely knew the guy. He went to a different school, and none of her friends knew him either.

They had met at a ball game, shared a few sentences, and then he had simply blurted it out.

"Why don't you go to the concert with me Friday? Great music. I've got wheels."

What's a girl to do? He looked good enough, and he seemed nice enough. Sure, she didn't really know him, but let's face it, the boys weren't exactly lining up and fighting over who would take her out.

In ten minutes he would probably be knocking on the door. Quickly, Jenny tried to run over her sensibility list.

One, don't sit in the car with him; get out when it stops.

Two, don't go to his house or yours after the concert unless parents are home.

Three, tell him your curfew right away and keep it. Don't seem indecisive.

Four, be friendly but cool. Don't be too aloof and don't cling either.

Five, reject any plan that takes the two of you away from people.

Six, the object is not romance, but fun; don't get confused.

Seven, choose your tone of voice and words carefully to indicate whether you want to go out again or not.

If the date turns very bad and you think you need to get out of there immediately, say so. "I don't think this is working. I need to go home," should do it. I know several girls who have done this and terminated the date. You don't want to do this simply because the music is loud; but if you sense that this is a bad situation, bail out. Tell him you want to go home. Walk over and join some friends. Call your parents and get a ride. Never tolerate a deteriorating situation that you think could go bad, especially if it's already pretty bad.

All of us need wisdom. Talk to the Lord before a date and ask him to make you wise. Tell him you want to have a good time, but you don't want to be a fool. Ask God to help you know when and how to be cautious. You will find him a very practical God.

> For the LORD gives wisdom.
> *Proverbs 2:6*

Think It Over

1. Would you date a stranger?
2. Do you have a reality check or a list of cautions that you discuss with friends?
3. When you face an "iffy" situation, do you discuss it with God?

Give Up the Faith?

"Young people are certainly terrible these days."

"Teens are a lot worse than when we were their age."

"They don't seem to have much faith in anything."

"Teens are just interested in drugs, rock, and drinking. They aren't like we used to be."

Are teenagers really giving up their faith in God and running full speed toward destruction? Some of them are! The news is packed with stories about young people who are involved in murder, mayhem, and lawlessness. But they are just the ones who make the headlines. The fact is that many teens today are believers.

Several surveys suggest that young people maintain the same religious faith and religious practices as their parents. As with each generation, the dress, vocabulary, and music tastes differ widely, but their belief systems are almost exactly the same.

A large percentage attend church, read their Bibles, pray, and believe that God loves them. According to one survey, over half the teens in this country attended church during the past month.

Knocking teens has become a sport. People in every generation have thought their youth were going to the dogs. But don't believe it. Young people are as loving, caring, and believing as in any other time in recent history.

When teens hear so much negative publicity, they begin to believe it. Some think "If teens are so bad, I must be terrible, too." Don't buy that junk. By the grace of God every teen is capable of being a fantastic person.

Don't think that young people have abandoned their faith in Jesus Christ. Never buy this picture that teens have become hordes of selfish pagans. That isn't the trend or the fad.

Go to a Christian concert, camp, or rally and see how many young people are enthusiastic about their living faith. See how many are being impacted by the Holy Spirit.

Teens as a whole have their heads screwed on pretty well, and many have a vital, vibrant faith in Christ. Many adults have seen the faith of young people, and they thank God for you.

For this reason, ever since I heard about your faith in the Lord Jesus and your love for all the saints, I have not stopped giving thanks for you, remembering you in my prayers.

Ephesians 1:15

Think It Over

1. How would you describe your faith in Christ?
2. Are you growing in your faith?
3. What do you do to help your faith grow?

Cheap Forgiveness

"It's really no big deal," Megan insisted. "After all God forgives me anyway."

Her attitude was borderline arrogant.

"Sure, I cheated. I'm not proud of that, but it happens all the time," she continued, almost smirking. "Everybody cheats some in school."

Did it bother her that she was a Christian who cheated?

"That's the magic," she smiled. "I'm already forgiven. I know Christ isn't excited about my copying a few answers, but it's no big sweat, either. He forgives me even before I do it. Not a bad deal, I figure."

Isn't Megan interested in obeying and pleasing God?

"Of course. But let's face it, no one's perfect. God understands I mess up. I can't worry all the time about doing wrong. I'd go psycho."

Like a lot of us, Megan has distorted the grace of God. Our first obligation before God is to obey. He expects us to follow him and do what is right. But because we sin and mess up, God offers us his forgiveness.

Christians should try not to sin. People who don't even try are rebelling against God. Forgiveness is not a license to do wrong. Forgiveness is the safety net when we sin.

When we sin because we can count on forgiveness, we are trying to manipulate God. If we plan to do something wrong *because* we are part of God's family, we are abusing that relationship.

First things first.

32

Our goal as children of God is to resist evil. God expects us to fight sin and aim for the good. A Christian who cheats on a test should have first agonized, fought, and gone through a moral crisis, before falling into the sin. But those of us who give in without a twinge of conscience should wonder how much spiritual life we really have.

The good news, however, does remain the same: God's forgiveness is available even to the most cold-hearted of us sinners. But it is an abuse of God's love to treat forgiveness as our free pass to do anything we want.

Read 1 John 2:1 and notice the order and emphasis:

My dear children, I write this to you so that you will not sin. But if anybody does sin, we have one who speaks to the Father in our defense—Jesus Christ, the Righteous One.

Think It Over

1. Sometimes do you feel callous about sin?
2. Have you ever planned to do something wrong because you knew God would forgive you?
3. Have you ever cried because you sinned?

Peaceful Solutions

Young people are turning to violence more than ever before in an attempt to settle differences. Most teenagers have seen violence increase in their neighborhoods and schools. It looks like we have forgotten how to resolve our problems in peaceful ways and are now determined to hurt each other.

One city in the Midwest reports that violent crime among teens has multiplied during the past ten years.

Felony assaults doubled.
Misdemeanor assaults quadrupled.
Rapes doubled.
Murders tripled.

Violent crimes among youth have grown much more rapidly than among adults. The causes may be many, but the cure could be simple. Christ taught us to avoid violence. Don't look for harmful ways to settle arguments with neighbors and friends. Even courtrooms are not the best places to resolve differences.

Peaceful solutions are the only acceptable way for people to work out their grievances. They need to talk, discuss, negotiate, and give and take. The best solutions are not suing, hitting, attacking, smashing, injuring, or getting even.

Our value systems have become so confused and weak that we think we need to hurt someone. Nothing could be further from the truth of the gospel of Jesus Christ. He taught us to:

Turn the other cheek.
Go the second mile.
Give our coat.

These are the ways of peace and not of violence. Not everyone is willing to accept the teaching of Jesus Christ, but those of us who do must reject violence. He told us to become peacemakers and not violence-makers.

When we have problems getting along with people, we need to solve those problems when they first start. Otherwise, the hostilities could grow, and our anger could get out of control. We need to use our verbal skills, our reasoning abilities, our intelligence, and our spiritual values to resolve the difficulties.

Christians do not have to resort to violence in order to work out relationships. Our strength comes from the Lord, and he can help us find peaceful solutions.

Settle matters quickly with your adversary who is taking you to court. Do it while you are still with him on the way, or he may hand you over to the judge, and the judge may hand you over to the officers, and you may be thrown into prison.

Matthew 5:25

Think It Over

1. Do you sometimes get violent at school or with your siblings?
2. Would you like to discuss your violence with a minister, teacher, parent, or counselor?
3. Ask the Lord to help make you more verbal and less violent.

Learning to Listen

There are several kinds of listening. Let's look at two of them.

One type of listening is to collect information and respond appropriately. A person tells me not to leave my guitar on the porch. If it rains, he explains, the wood could warp, and the instrument might never play right again.

I hear that. I think it sounds reasonable. I agree that it would be a dumb act to leave a guitar out in the open.

The second type of listening is to hear what is said but fail to *listen*. I leave the guitar on the porch. During the night it rains, and the guitar gets wet.

The question is, did I listen or did I listen?

Smart people listen to their parents, as in type one listening. They collect information.

Their parents say:

Don't leave the meat out.
Save some money for college.
Put mothballs in your closet.
Don't drink and drive.

Even if they don't obey, smart people listen to what their parents have to say. It's really dumb to simply shrug off parents' words and totally ignore them.

God gave us parents so they could teach us—among many other reasons. If we close our ears and don't even take in the information, we miss a lot of things we need to know.

Smart teens listen. Really smart teens *listen* and also do what needs to be done. If they refuse to obey, they often end up in more trouble than they can handle.

Teens like to pull away from their parents. But only fools pull too far. God gave us parents partly to keep us out of trouble.

> Listen, my son, and be wise, and keep your heart on the right path.
>
> *Proverbs 23:19*

Think It Over

1. Do you sometimes act like your parents don't know anything?
2. When you do listen to your parents, is it type one listening or type two?
3. Have you ever thanked God for what your parents say?

Don't Be Discouraged

Craig MacFarlene is a very active person. He is heavily involved in wrestling, snow skiing, waterskiing, golf, and track and field events. He plays eleven instruments and is a public speaker.

All of that would be remarkable enough, but it is even more impressive because Craig is blind. He has not been able to see since he was two years old.

Over the years many people tried to discourage this young Canadian. They probably didn't want to see him get hurt or have his feelings crushed. But Craig's outstanding attitude and determination have sent him on to speak at two Republican National Conventions.

His story is enough to make us take a second look at our own disabilities. Some of us aren't tall enough, fast enough, or coordinated enough to make our dreams come true. At least that's what we think until we hear a story like Craig's.

Too often we concentrate on what we think our disabilities are, and we become discouraged. Most teens can accomplish far more than they think they can.

There was a football player with only part of one foot.
There have been one-armed and one-legged baseball players.
There are writers who can't type.
Some singers can barely sing.
Bo Jackson has an artificial hip.
There are inventors who had trouble in school.
There have been presidents who lost elections over and over again.
There are beautiful girls who never had dates in school.

Many C students have become A students.
Some great missionaries were rejected by mission boards.
Many students who were told they weren't "college material"
  now have doctorate degrees.

We can't let our disabilities discourage us. They are obstacles,
but obstacles can be overcome.

God didn't create us to pout over what we can't do. He made
us to make the most of what we can do. God doesn't want us to
emphasize our disabilities but to specialize in our abilities.

Don't be discouraged.
Don't be discouraged.
Don't be discouraged.

Have I not commanded you? Be strong and courageous.
Do not be terrified; do not be discouraged, for the Lord your
God will be with you wherever you go.

Joshua 1:9

Think It Over

1. What would you do if you could?
2. Are you willing to try it?
3. Ask God to help you try it.

When You're Really Rattled

You've seen large street-cleaning equipment that is driven along the street curbs. It has huge vacuum hoses, and its job is to pick up leaves. The machine also collects dirt, debris, and whatever else is lying around.

One of these machines went rumbling down the street in a New England city. As it sucked up a pile of leaves, an unexpected lump got pulled into the cleaner. At 175 miles an hour a small orange and white kitten was inhaled into the loud, vibrating machine.

"Usually anything that goes in there is pretty much history," one of the workers explained.

The poor kitten was rescued from the machine, but it looked like it had stuck its paw into a light socket. Its hair stood straight out, its eyes bulged, and its mouth was crooked. Fortunately some kind people adopted the frazzled little creature and gave it a home. Rumor has it that they called the kitten Hoover.

None of us has made the big trip through a vacuum cleaner, though some days we feel like we have. Teachers are on our case, parents are carping about everything, the coach just called us a roach, our math grade dropped to F-, and our hair went into rebellion. Our world hasn't fallen apart, but the seams are showing stress.

Where do you go to calm down? How do you stop the machine of life from shaking so you can get some peace?

Have you ever tried giving it to God one piece at a time?

🐾 the teacher
🐾 the coach
🐾 the parent
🐾 the friend
🐾 the hair
🐾 the little brother

Name them each—one by one—and ask the Lord to show you how to handle each situation. There is no need to feel alone as you get sucked up the hose of life.

By committing each person, each obstacle, each incident to him, you begin to take the rattle out. When the vibrating ends, you can go on with confidence and find strength in God's Holy Spirit.

The Lord reigns, let the nations tremble; he sits enthroned between the cherubim, let the earth shake.

Psalm 99:1

Think It Over

1. What do you usually do when you feel totally rattled?
2. Can you look at your problems one at a time instead of as a bunch?
3. Can you lay them out one at a time and ask the Lord to help you with them?

Who Controls Us?

Don't you hate it when your parents tell you what to do? "Turn that off"; "get that done"; "call your grandmother." It makes you feel like a little kid.

Let's put a stop to it. Imagine your dad walking into your room and saying he is taking his hands off. From now on he is willing to let you totally run your own life. No more prodding, pulling, or pushing.

How would that affect your life? Would your parents' refusal to interfere make your life better or worse?

Would you eat breakfast?
Would you ever turn off the TV?
Would you do your homework?
Would your grades plummet?
Would fuzz grow on your carpet?
Would fungus breed on your gym socks?
Would you join a motorcycle gang?
Would the volume of your CD player cause the walls to tremble?
Would every cop in town know you by your first name?

Some teens have grown up to be outstanding adults, even though they had almost no parental control. Others, without adult supervision, are now serving time in prison. Which way do you think your disk would flop?

The best way to find out is to exercise self-control now. How good are you at getting things done? How often do you take care of your things before your parents go ballistic?

Too many of us are like mules. If someone doesn't get a stick out, we are too stubborn to do anything. But there are exceptions, and maybe you are one of them.

Take control and responsibility for your own life. Stay one step ahead, and you can cut way down on the amount of supervision that goes on.

People who drive mules by cracking whips and shouting are called mule skinners. We aren't animals, and we can do what needs to be done before the mule skinner shows up.

Do not be like the horse or the mule, which have no understanding but must be controlled by bit and bridle or they will not come to you.

Psalm 32:9

Think It Over

1. Are you a self-starter?
2. Are you in the habit of waiting for your parents to tell you what to do?
3. Would you like to talk to God about taking more self-control?

Jesus Is Lord

I was watching an action movie complete with guns, car chases, and razor-sharp arrows screaming across the screen. In the middle of all that chaos a woman on the screen hurriedly used a telephone to seek information. On the side of the phone was pasted a piece of yellow paper with the words, "Jesus is Lord."

For what seemed like minutes the camera stared at the lady, the telephone, and the sign. The message beamed at millions of moviegoers all over the country.

What does that mean? Is Jesus really the

Lord of the universe?
Lord of the world?
Lord of the unseen world?
Lord of my life?

The answer to all four of those questions is yes. The most important question, though, is: Do you accept the lordship of Jesus Christ?

Lordship means someone has authority. We don't use the term much anymore, but a person who owns a ranch is lord of the estate. He has authority over everything that happens on his property.

The fact is that Jesus is Lord over everything and everyone. Our task is to admit that Jesus is in charge and surrender to his authority. If we do that, we accept Jesus' lordship.

If we rebel against his authority, we are fighting reality. It's like saying we reject gravity. Gravity doesn't depend on our willingness to accept or deny it. Gravity will remain gravity no matter what we think.

Jesus will remain Lord. The note by the phone has it right. Jesus Christ has total authority. "Do I want to submit myself to his authority or lordship?" is the real question.

Rain is a fact. When it rains, the rain doesn't particularly care what I think about it. I can ignore, defy, resist, or rebel against the rain if I choose. I may walk in the rain with a hat, umbrella, or jacket and reject the rain. What will happen? The rain keeps coming, and I will get wet.

Jesus is Lord. The more I accept that fact, the more I walk in harmony with reality. Accept and admit the lordship of Jesus and live in oneness with him.

Thomas said to him, "My Lord and my God!"
John 20:28

Think It Over

1. Does it help to know that Jesus has authority over everything?
2. Do you have trouble submitting to his control and authority?
3. Ask God to increase your sense of well-being as you accept his authority and control.

Do You Need a Drink?

Take a quick test to see how you rate alcohol.

1. Do you need a drink to get ready for a test?
2. Do you feel socially inadequate without a drink?
3. Are you funnier after you drink?
4. Do you think you are better at sports after you have a drink?
5. Do you think drinking doesn't affect your driving?
6. Does it take a drink to relax you?
7. Do you think you are more appealing after you have a drink?
8. Will you get invited to more things if you are willing to have a drink?
9. If one drink is good for you, are two drinks better?
10. Do you drink alcohol alone?

If some of these things are true of you, you could be in danger of developing a drinking problem. Be smart. Talk to someone about it.

Wine is a mocker and beer a brawler; whoever is led astray by them is not wise.

Proverbs 20:1

Think It Over

1. What decisions have you made about alcohol?
2. Are you presently drinking illegally?
3. How many of the ten questions sound like you?

Man Bites Mosquito

You aren't going to believe this story. You've heard strange tales before, but this one is going to challenge your imagination.

Near Little Rock, Arkansas, a group of people gather every year just to eat mosquitoes. They call it the Mosquito Cook-off.

You've probably heard of Rattlesnake Days where people catch rattlesnakes, cook them, and eat them. Maybe you've even heard of eating chocolate-covered ants. But are you ready for mosquito chip cookies?

If this appeals to you at all, be sure to order the mosquito cookbook. In the meantime start collecting mosquitoes. Most recipes call for at least a quarter-cup of mosquitoes. They will need to be cooked for thirty minutes; but surely the details will be spelled out in the cookbook.

Those who have eaten mosquitoes regularly tell us the dry ones are the best. Evidently fresh mosquitoes taste too gummy. Does this sound strange? Actually there isn't anything wrong with being strange. It sounds like some people are having a lot of fun in Arkansas.

Strange can be good. It all depends on what we are strange about. If strange means we don't get drunk, let's be strange. If strange means we don't hurt people, let's be strange. If strange means we are fair and loving and serve God, let's go for the strange. If strange means we don't steal, hate, kill, spread AIDS, or abandon children, maybe that's what we want to be. If strange means we follow Christ and praise God, how bad can that be?

Many times we are treated like we are strange simply because we live the Christian life. We've always been treated that way. Let's keep on being strange if that's what it takes to follow Christ.

For you have spent enough time in the past doing what pagans choose to do—living in debauchery, lust, drunkenness, orgies, carousing and detestable idolatry. They think it strange that you do not plunge with them into the same flood of dissipation, and they heap abuse on you.

1 Peter 4:3–4

Think It Over

1. Would you eat a mosquito chip cookie?
2. How are you "strange" compared to the non-Christians around you?
3. Have you ever asked Christ to give you strength in your "strangeness"?

Facts about Teens

This may be a great time to be a teenager. There are many opportunities. There is less war; advances are being made in medicine; electronic miracles are being accomplished in computers, music, and other fields. Young people could and should have a bright future with many years of happiness and accomplishments.

But there are also many obstacles along the way—big, ugly, dangerous problems all around. This is what's happening to teens today in record numbers:

Sexual diseases of all kinds are rising sharply.
Teen pregnancies are skyrocketing.
Arrests of youths continue to climb.
A lower percentage of teens graduate from high school.
The death rate among teens is increasing.
Alcoholism is more prevalent.
Drugs are widely available.
One-half of teens have single parents, divorced parents, and
    stepparents.

It's more fun to list all of the good things that teens have going for them, but sometimes the sick list has to be compiled, too. There are many ditches to fall into and many stones to trip over.

Sometimes we dig our own pits, and then we fall into them. We mess around with crime just for the excitement. We try some sex, and we are foolish. We have to experiment with drugs simply to say we did.

50

That's like digging holes. We think only others ever fall into them. But some day we might dig a hole and then turn around and stumble into it.

We can't blame others for all the bad things that come our way. Often we set our own traps.

If a man digs a pit, he will fall into it; if a man rolls a stone, it will roll back on him.

Proverbs 26:27

Think It Over

1. Do you feel that you might be digging a hole somehow right now?
2. Why do you keep digging?
3. Would you like to ask God to give you the courage to back off before you fall in?

Snakes in the Jungle

Laughed At

Tracey didn't like to let people know she was a Christian. When other teens found out, one or two would always make fun of her. Her faith in Christ was terribly important, and Tracey hated to be kidded about it.

"Watch your language; here comes Mother Tracey," one of them would joke.

"Help me, Jesus," another teen chirped as he passed her in the hall.

No one ever took a swing at her or dumped her books out of a window, but the remarks were annoying. The teasing upset her, and she felt embarrassed.

When Tracey first entered high school, she decided to turn over a new leaf. She made a real effort to blend in and not say anything about her beliefs. Soon she learned that she couldn't hide it very well.

Marshall's father was in a serious car accident, and Tracey told him she would pray for his dad.

When Reed was teased because he had an accent, Tracey invited him to her youth group.

Heather was depressed a lot over her family situation, and Tracey brought her a New Testament.

Tracey wanted to cover up her Christianity. She had seen other teens do it, but she found it too hard to pretend.

"Pray for me, sister. I've got a tough geometry exam," a friend half kidded as they entered school together.

"Don't forget. If you want to smoke something that will give you a real religious experience, let me know," another student chimed in.

No one likes to be laughed at. But sometimes Tracey knew it was a small price to pay. What was she to do? she wondered. Not help people, not pray for people, not live like a Christian? That was too much to ask.

No one ever arrested Tracey for her faith. They didn't throw her out of school. No one ever threatened her life. Tracey was respected, treated fairly, and liked by most students. When she thought about those who had been tortured, murdered, deported, and hated for their faith, Tracey realized how easy it was to take a few jokes and blush a little.

In your struggle against sin, you have not yet resisted to the point of shedding your blood.

Hebrews 12:4

Think It Over

1. Name ten friends; how many of them know you are a Christian?
2. Are you teased much for your faith?
3. Is there some situation where you should show more of your faith in Christ?

Cults and False Christs

A group of religious people sold all of their possessions—their cars, their furniture, and their homes—and got together, waiting for the return of Christ. Their leader told them what day he thought Jesus would come back, and they all met on a hill to pray.

Morning came and went. Afternoon wasted away. The night was chilly and still. When the sun rose the next morning, everyone was sitting around with no sign of Christ.

Don't you wish you could have been there to hear the leader explain? How did he mess up so badly? But he probably kept most of his followers. For some reason they don't give up. Before long he probably set a new date, or else went on to chase some other religious project.

Groups like this are often confusing to people like us. Sometimes their actions rattle our faith just a little. If these believers can act so foolishly, we wonder, is our faith this foolish too?

Fortunately, Jesus Christ told us this would happen. We shouldn't get upset when others claim to carry special messages from God or call themselves the Christ. False christs come and go, and they always have.

Don't be fooled.
Don't get discouraged.
Don't get confused.
Don't give up.

Be steady. Follow the Christ of the Bible and only the Christ of the Bible. Refuse to follow popular leaders or the newest fad in religion. Anyone who claims to have special messages from

God is not to be trusted. God gave us the Bible to lead us, and we look to it for direction.

It's true that God may lead people or even give them special messages. We can't limit God's ability to do whatever he chooses. But that message can only be for the person who receives it. Don't let someone say that God gave him a message for you. It's too dangerous to have people leading us around and claiming that God told them to do it.

Never follow a phony christ. Stick with the Christ of the Scriptures.

Jesus answered: "Watch out that no one deceives you. For many will come in my name, claiming, 'I am the Christ,' and will deceive many."

Matthew 24:4–5

Think It Over

1. Have you ever felt confused by the stories about cult leaders and followers?
2. How do you handle it?
3. Have you invited the real Christ into your life? What guidelines help you follow him?

Head Shaving

Don't answer this one lightly: Would you be willing to shave your head completely bald for a friend?

In Yorkville, Illinois, a thirteen-year-old boy named Mark was undergoing treatment for leukemia. The chemotherapy treatment was causing the eighth-grader to lose his hair.

Someone who is bald and in the eighth grade is likely to stand out. Students might stare. The person could become self-conscious. Thoughtless teens might yell "cue-ball" or "glass-top," or just plain "baldy."

One of Mark's friends decided to help. He and fourteen other students got their heads shaved bald, too. It was hard to tell who had leukemia and who had gotten a serious buzz job.

Before the teens jumped in, they showed the maturity to get it all checked out beforehand. First, they got Mark's approval. They didn't want him to think they were making fun of him. The students also showed enough sense to ask the school principal what she thought. Evidently she thought the boys should wear hats to class to keep the chill off their bald heads.

It isn't easy to identify with others who are under stress. Often we are so busy fighting our own battles that we don't take time to think about others. But sometimes we do. And sometimes the greatest stories and the best examples are about teenagers.

Teens who go and sit with the person who is being picked on.
Teens who meet the new student and make him feel welcome.
Teens who invite the girl with the reputation to church.
Teens who refuse to gay-bash.
Teens who don't judge people by their clothes.

58

These things happen all the time. They may not be as dramatic as shaving heads. They may not make national news. But brave, thoughtful, caring teenagers take risks to help each other because they can be tremendously kind.

Blessed is he who is kind to the needy.
Proverbs 14:21

Think It Over

1. Can you think of a time when teens have sacrificed to help another teen?
2. Is there someone at school or church who could use special attention right now?
3. Is there a situation that your youth group might help? (You don't have to shave heads.)

Settling Differences

This reads like a typical newspaper article that would appear on page three or four.

Two former friends were arguing over a CD player. They each had contributed money to its purchase but lately had fought over who was using it the most.

Friday night, after yet another heated exchange, teen A went home and got his parents' handgun. Returning to teen B's home, he shot teen B at close range and killed him. Teen A then carried the CD player to his own house. Police arrested teen A without incident.

This type of story is being reported all over the country. Simply fill in the names and change the reason for the dispute, and something like this has probably happened where each of us live.

Don't people know how to argue anymore? Have we forgotten how to settle our differences? Are we so uptight and frustrated that we have to get a weapon simply to make a point?

Jesus Christ taught us to solve our problems with people before they escalate into violence. He told us that if someone is upset at us, we should go and see him. Christ didn't tell us to take a spear or a bow and arrow or a large rock in case the discussion didn't go well. Neither did he suggest we take along a handful of friends to back us up.

The Son of God wasn't talking about intimidation or force or any form of violence. The goal was to settle our differences, not to cause an explosion.

He told us to stop what we are doing—whether we are doing homework, shooting hoops, or whatever. Even if we are sitting in church praying, we should get up, go see the person, and work it out.

If we don't settle our differences with words, what will we do? Without discussion, compromise, and understanding, what choices do we have? By removing words as tools, too many are turning to weapons. Resolving differences with weapons is new among teens. In previous generations youthful debates might have been concluded by a fistfight but almost never with guns.

Lower the heat while you still can. Make peace with every person before someone gets hurt.

Therefore, if you are offering your gift at the altar and there remember that your brother has something against you, leave your gift there in front of the altar. First go and be reconciled to your brother; then come and offer your gift.

Matthew 5:23–24

Think It Over

1. Is there someone you need to make peace with?
2. Are you willing to go to him one more time?
3. If you feel you can't go to him, is there someone else you could discuss the problem with?

Lying Lips

It seems almost silly to discuss lying. Dishonesty is so widespread and socially accepted, why bother trying to fight it? We still need to hash the subject around because it's wrong, and so much damage is done by lying.

Ask yourself if you would lie under these circumstances:

Would you lie on a job application in order to get hired?

Would you lie to your parents?

Would you lie to an insurance company in order to receive more money?

Would you lie to a girlfriend or boyfriend?

Would you lie to get a college loan?

If pulled over by a policeman, would you lie to avoid getting a ticket?

If you owned a business, would you lie to the customers?

Would you lie on your income tax form?

These are situations that most of us will face. It's not the same as asking if you would lie to the enemy during wartime. Each of us must decide whether we will lie because it's easy, or if we will resist the practice because it's wrong and harmful.

Many of us would avoid problems for ourselves and for others if we simply accepted an honesty policy. The Ten Commandments have taught us for thousands of years not to bear false witness against our neighbors.

Why do we lie?

Because we are afraid of the truth.

Because we are greedy.

Because we want to cheat people.
Because we feel insecure.
Because we are sinners.

There must be many explanations. Some people even lie when it would be easier to tell the truth.

Christians need to take a strong stand in their own hearts against lying. The truth serves both God and people better than lies.

The LORD detests lying lips, but he delights in men who are truthful.

Proverbs 12:22

Are You Bored?

Is that what's bothering you, Bunky?

Do you spend your evenings raiding the fridge and watching home shopping?

Have you started a dustball collection, and you have no one to show it to?

Is your best friend a stuffed teddy bear with one eye missing and a tongue that has turned pink?

When you go away, do you send postcards to yourself?

Have you started to name the water bugs in your basement?

Is this your idea of a hot evening: Crush cookies on the counter and suck up the crumbs with a straw?

If this sounds like your life video, this is what you need to do, Bunky. Call the hospital—not the psycho ward but the volunteer department. Tell them you want to work one evening a week. Let them know you are willing to carry flowers, push wheelchairs, pick up trays, visit with patients, whatever.

You may have to be thirteen or fourteen to qualify. Expect to take a short orientation class. In some cases you have to maintain a C average at school. There could be a waiting list to get in, but maybe not.

If you are near a soup kitchen, a homeless shelter, or a child care center, these would be good places to plug in also. Take the opportunity to help others. You might even meet other teens. Hanging around the house like a lump is a serious downer. Idleness can make a person feel dismal.

It's risky. Volunteer work may cause you to neglect your algae collection in the bathtub. You may have to say good-bye to your favorite TV show, "Lost Parasites of the Amazon." You might have to leave half of the cream cakes uneaten.

But it won't be boring, Bunky.

> And at evening let not your hands be idle.
>
> *Ecclesiastes 11:6*

Think It Over

1. Would you like to find someone who needs you?
2. Are you sometimes bored and lonely?
3. Where could you volunteer to help others?

Are You What You Eat?

The geometrid caterpillar is. It has the ability to change and look like its food. You can stare at a pile of twigs and not be able to tell which is the twig and which is the caterpillar.

The ones that eat flowers from trees grow sacs, turn yellow and grow tufts, just like the flower. Those that eat leaves become green-gray, straighten out, and develop small bumps like twigs.

Members of the geometrid family will look different even though they live in the same tree. One caterpillar may eat the flowers and be one color and shape. Cousin caterpillar eats only leaves and becomes a different color and shape than its relative.

Those changes in appearance work very well to fool birds. Birds fly around looking for juicy caterpillars to eat or to take back to their nests. Even if a bird lands on a branch of the tree and stares right at this caterpillar, it will have trouble figuring out if it's a twig for the nest or food.

God intended that Christians become like the geometrid caterpillar. Not that we eat leaves and turn green, or conform to our food, but that we change. God wants us to become more and more like the person he created us to be.

Each of us is part of God's purpose. God wants Christians to become more Christ-like. He wants us to serve and worship him. He wants us to reach out and help others in the name of God. He also wants us to be led by the Holy Spirit so that God can work in our lives daily.

The problem is that many Christians eat only from non-Christian trees. That makes us look and act like nonbelievers. We don't exercise our faith. We fail to stay God-conscious. We become selfish and greedy, all because we are munching on the wrong leaves.

God wants us to be part of his purpose and will. In order to do that, we have to spend time communicating with God and feeding on his Word.

In a spiritual sense, we are what we eat.

In him we were also chosen, having been predestined according to the plan of him who works out everything in conformity with the purpose of his will.

Ephesians 1:11

Think It Over

1. How are you becoming like the people around you?
2. Are the people around you becoming like you?
3. Do you see yourself becoming more interested in the things that are of interest to God?

Poisonous Like a Snake

How do you know if you have been bitten by a poisonous snake? Sometimes you don't know. A poisonous snake can bite and not inject any poison. You could put your hand into a pile of rocks and feel a sharp bite but never know what it was.

If the massasauga rattlesnake bites and injects poison, there are some definite signs. When the venom goes into a person's hand, the hand may swell to twice its size. As the poison travels, it pushes at the nerves and causes terrible pain.

Most people live following snake bites, but a doctor's care is usually required. The Bible compares wine with a bite from a poisonous snake. It says that people who spend too much time with wine could get hurt badly.

A large number of teenagers drink alcohol occasionally or regularly. The truth is that most teenagers drink to some extent, and none of them think alcohol is going to be a problem. Teens are confident when it comes to taking risks. They don't like to listen to adults, and they usually shrug off advice, especially when it comes to alcohol.

It would help if teenagers would only wait to drink; they can make decisions about alcohol when they get out of school. But they seem afraid—afraid they will miss something—afraid they will be left out—afraid they won't have enough fun.

With so many other big decisions to make, it's unfortunate that young people get pushed into the alcohol decision, too. Grades, careers, schools, friends, and dating are all heavy issues.

Some teenagers do make the decision to put alcohol on hold. Although they are accepted and respected, they have decided not to cloud their lives with the complications of alcohol. It works for them.

Alcohol carries a terrible bite. It makes some people do things they would otherwise never do. Alcohol also addicts some people, and they may never throw it off.

Every person must make his or her own decision. But all of us should know that alcohol has fangs.

Do not gaze at wine when it is red, when it sparkles in the cup, when it goes down smoothly! In the end it bites like a snake and poisons like a viper.

Proverbs 23:31–32

Think It Over

1. Why do teens drink alcohol?
2. How do you feel about it?
3. Would you like the Lord to help you resist it during your teen years? Why not tell him how you feel?

Commandments for Parents

If you could make a list of commandments that parents should follow, what would be on the list? This is my list.

1. Thou shalt love your teen on good days and on bad.
2. Thou shalt share your value system with teens so they can have a foundation to stand on.
3. Thou shalt be willing to listen and learn from your teens, especially about their culture, pressures, and happiness.
4. Thou shalt never shout at your teen when you can speak softly.
5. Thou shalt trust your teen but not all of the time.
6. Thou shalt be slow to bash your teenager's friends.
7. Thou shalt not take lightly what your teen takes seriously.
8. Thou shalt model your faith for your teen.
9. Thou shalt not make your teen the center of your life.
10. Thou shalt give your teens responsibilities and let them experience the consequences.
11. Thou shalt praise your teen every chance you get.
12. Thou shalt ask the Lord to watch over, protect, and care for your teens.

Think It Over

These commandments aren't chiseled in stone, so they can be changed. How would you change my list? Which commandments would you add?

Commandments for Teens

Suppose you could make a list of commandments as to how teens should deal with their parents. I've made a list. You feel free to add or subtract and make your own choices.

1. Thou shalt communicate instead of clamming up.
2. Thou shalt accept your parents as they are and not be embarrassed by them.
3. Thou shalt go cheerfully on some trips with the family just to maintain relationships.
4. Thou shalt not rebel so drastically because it's hard to heal later.
5. Thou shalt not look at yourself as the most important part of the universe.
6. Thou shalt not reject everything your parents say or do.
7. Thou shalt not scream "Nobody cares about me around here" and stomp out of the room more than once a week.
8. Thou shalt not bring any friend over to the house who actually chews on furniture.
9. Thou shalt praise your parents twice a week.
10. Thou shalt pray for a better attitude toward your parents.
11. Thou shalt give some thought to the problems your parents may be going through.
12. Thou shalt work at telling your parents where you are going and when you might be back.

Think It Over

This is just a starter list. Change it around and make up your own list of commandments.

The Runaway Turtle

Sexual Harassment

Maybe it's worse today, but it has always been around. Making sexual remarks, poking fun about people's bodies, grabbing, pinching, brushing up against people in the hall. A recent study suggests that 85 percent of the girls and 76 percent of the boys in the survey reported being sexually harassed as teenagers.

And it isn't restricted to young people. In some job situations a great deal of sexual teasing goes on among adults.

Some people laugh at the idea. They don't understand how anyone can be harmed with a little sexual "fun." But when we think it over, the pain and agony become obvious.

Self-conscious teenage girls don't want to be made fun of because their breasts are too small or too large. No one wants to stand up in class and have a couple of boys in the back begin to make "moo" sounds. Girls don't want to have their blouses grabbed in the hall or their anatomy patted as they walk by.

Sexual harassment is a form of intimidation. Girls are often afraid to walk alone, speak up in class, or wear anything but the loosest of clothing. They get the feeling that many guys are simply creeps who violate anyone they choose.

What's a Christian to do? How can we show respect for people of either sex?

Ask the Lord to help you control a few things.

1. Try not to laugh at sexual jokes, particularly when they embarrass other people.
2. Never join in by making sounds of ridicule.

3. Discourage younger teens from sexual harassment. Tell thirteen-year-olds that the practice is dumb. They often respect older teens.
4. Keep your hands to yourself.

The people who will have the biggest impact on sexual harassment are other teens. Young people do it because it is acceptable; they will stop doing it when it is not acceptable.

Show proper respect to everyone.
1 Peter 2:17

Think It Over

1. Is there someone you need to stop making fun of?
2. Can you befriend someone who is being sexually harassed?
3. Is there a younger person you could discourage from the practice?

Teen Court

In Ames, Iowa, an experiment has been conducted using teenagers to sentence teenagers in county court. A jury of young people decides what punishment should be meted out to youthful offenders.

Not every teen can be sentenced by teen court. They have to meet certain criteria.

1. The person usually has no previous criminal record.
2. The crime must be minor.
3. The teen has confessed to the crime.

Teen court is not a bag of hot air. The jurors hand down serious sentences that can require up to three months' time to be served.

One teen, arrested for public intoxication, was sentenced to pick up trash on Saturday mornings. He also was placed on two months' probation and had to submit regular blood tests.

The experiment is based on the theory that teens understand teens. They know the temptations, weaknesses, and pitfalls that young people face. However, that doesn't mean teen jurors are more lenient in their sentencing. I served on a college committee selected to determine what restrictions should be placed on failing students. The students on the committee were much harsher than the school administration would have been.

It's difficult to be judged fairly. No one knows exactly what motivates another person. And yet we have to have courts and judges, or else we wouldn't be able to live together in a peaceful society.

Fortunately the totally fair and caring judge is coming. That judge is Jesus Christ, the Son of God. Those of us who have believed in and accepted him as our Savior will find him a forgiving, loving, kind judge. He will not judge us on the basis of whether we were good or bad. All of us are sinners. Rather, he will judge us on whether or not we received God's Son as our Redeemer.

Are you ready if the judge should come today? Ask Christ to forgive you of your sins and to come into your life, and you can be ready.

Don't grumble against each other, brothers, or you will be judged. The Judge is standing at the door!

James 5:9

Think It Over

1. Would you like to serve on a teen court?
2. Would you like to see a teen court at school?
3. Have you accepted Christ as your Savior and are you ready for the judge to come?

Wanted

Have you ever felt as if no one wanted you? You were having a bad day, the teacher barked, your parents growled, and a neighbor yelled because you walked across the grass. It may not happen every day, but sometimes the feelings of rejection pile up and make you feel like last week's trash.

The sense of not being wanted can make us do all sorts of dumb things. Often young people get into trouble simply because they think nobody cares what happens to them anyway.

At a panel discussing violence among teenagers, a community leader said young people need three things if they are to stay out of trouble.

1. They need education.
2. They need a schedule of noneducational activities.
3. They need someone to make them feel wanted.

Some parents want their teenagers, and, frankly, some parents don't. More parents want and love them than most teenagers realize; but they go through family turmoil and tension, and it seems like parents want to ship them off. So, every now and then they really may not feel loved or wanted.

There is one person who always wants us, everyday, under all conditions. That person is Jesus Christ, the Son of God. He isn't fickle or temperamental. Even when we treat him like day-old toast, he hangs in there and always wants us.

People can be moody. One day they act like we're special, and the next day they want to sic the dog on us. That's just normal for many of us. God isn't that way. He hangs out the wanted sign every day and he means it.

When you feel all alone in a beat-up, dented world, remember that someone still cares. Jesus Christ holds out his arms and wants you to come to him. He wants to include you in his family forever.

Come to me, all you who are weary and burdened, and I will give you rest.

Matthew 11:28

Think It Over

1. Have you accepted Jesus Christ's invitation to come to him?
2. Do you believe that Jesus is the Son of God?
3. Have you asked him to come into your life and forgive you of all your sins?

The Prayer Wall

Talking to God isn't like it used to be. Devoted Jews used to travel to Jerusalem to pray. They would leave prayer notes tucked inside the cracks of the Western Wall.

Today there is a service where you can fax your prayers to Jerusalem, and someone will stick the prayers in the holes. People still make the pilgrimage, but modern technology is speeding up the prayer process.

Many of us hit another kind of wall when we try to pray. It's more like a brick wall. Have you ever started to talk to God, but the words wouldn't come out? Your mind begins to rev with a thousand thoughts, but you still don't know what to say.

For the moment you feel:

- guilty
- bewildered
- unworthy
- defeated
- confused
- inadequate
- all of the above

Words won't flow. Your brain cells smash into each other like a huge traffic jam. You suffer from major tongue failure. Let's call it prayer-block. You want to pray, you have the best of intentions, but you've hit the big wall.

I suffer from it all the time. Sometimes I can deal with it, and sometimes I can't.

80

One of the best ways to handle prayer-block is to back up. Stop trying so hard to force it. Relax. Stop staring at yourself and your own inadequacy.

For one solid minute simply praise God. Thank God for every good thing you can think of: friends, family, health, youth group, Jesus, contact lenses, food, computers, clothes, telephones, anything and everything. Name the small, everyday stuff, and include the big, special things. Free-float and mention whatever comes to mind.

Congratulations! You broke prayer-block. If that's all you got done today, you've accomplished a lot. You ran into a large, thick wall, but you didn't let it stop you. You turned a negative downer into a positive communication with God.

This could change the entire tone of your day. Maybe God has answered the prayer that you had trouble praying.

So that in all things God may be praised through Jesus Christ. To him be the glory and the power for ever and ever. Amen.

1 Peter 4:11

Think It Over

1. When is the best time for you to pray? Why?
2. Why do you pray? Can you think of three reasons?
3. Have you ever thanked God for something that went wrong? Like what?

They Stood Up

When the United States Supreme Court ruled against some forms of prayer at high school graduations, many adults began to tremble. If the court put limitations on prayer, school boards weren't going to mess with it. All across the country prayer was dropped like a cinder block, and many people hid from the issue.

But not teenagers. Far from being afraid, many high school seniors decided to stand up for their beliefs. In one high school a moment of silence was included in the graduation program. When that time came, many of the seniors joined in unison and recited the Lord's Prayer aloud.

At another school one of the seniors used his turn to speak as an opportunity to lead in prayer. School board members were shocked, but most people appreciated it.

The students in a town in Iowa took legal action. They asked a court to give them permission to pray at graduation. The court agreed, and the students carried through with their plan.

Christian young people shouldn't go to war with adults or school boards or authority. Most of the time they need to comply. However, there are times and certain situations when teenagers should stand up for what they believe.

They can do it politely. They can do it properly. They can do it lovingly. But they need to do it.

If their faith is ridiculed in class, they may need to object. If their morals are made fun of, they may need to say something. If they are asked to believe something that they don't feel is true, they should protest. If they are forced to participate in rituals or practices that they consider ungodly, they need to take a stand.

Don't look for trouble, but don't be afraid either. Every Christian should take a stand for his or her beliefs when these beliefs are threatened.

Be on your guard; stand firm in the faith; be men of courage; be strong. Do everything in love.

1 Corinthians 16:13–14

Think It Over

1. Can you think of a time when you had to take a stand because of your beliefs?
2. Do you have friends who try to pull you away from your Christian values? Explain.
3. How do you resist when friends try to pull you away?

Get Your Watch Out

Pick up your Bible and turn to Matthew 6. Go ahead and do it. I'll wait. Now get a clock that counts seconds, and place the clock where you can easily see it.

The assignment is to read verses 9 through 13 — but don't start yet. This passage of Scripture is the famous Lord's Prayer. We recite this prayer in many churches and in some schools.

Jesus Christ prayed the prayer on the Mount of Olives. He gave it as a model prayer. This is the way we are supposed to talk to God. This prayer has helped countless millions of people for centuries.

When you read the prayer this time, clock yourself. How long does it take to read verses 9 through 13? Do that part of the assignment now.

Were you surprised at the time? Do it again just to make sure. How long did it take the second time?

Usually it takes thirty-five to forty seconds to read or recite the Lord's Prayer. What does that tell us? Was Jesus pressed for time, so he prayed short? Did Matthew run out of room, so he recorded only part of the prayer? Or did Jesus Christ believe in the power of a short, direct prayer?

There are reasons to pray for a long time. There could be a great many things to talk to God about. The person praying might be deeply earnest and want to plead with God. How long we pray is our concern.

But we don't have to pray for a long time. There's no need to feel like a failure if we talk to God for thirty-five seconds. Good, brief conversations are often the most meaningful. They are to the point and helpful.

And when you pray, do not keep on babbling like pagans,
for they think they will be heard because of their many words.

Matthew 6:7

Think It Over

1. Do you usually pray longer than thirty-five seconds or
   shorter?
2. What is one of your favorite one-sentence prayers?
3. How often do you pray for four minutes or more? What
   causes you to pray longer?

The Faith Killer

A survey was taken of people who gave up their religion. In some cases they may have given up their personal beliefs, too, but basically they were the ones who stopped practicing their religion. They no longer attended services or were part of a religious group.

Several reasons were given for their change. One of the most frequent causes listed was because of the person they married. Their spouse didn't share the same beliefs, want to attend church, or care to engage in the same practices.

It probably didn't take a survey for most of us to figure that one out. If your husband or wife throws cold water on your faith in Christ, it will be harder for you to keep the fires burning.

That's one of the reasons that it is important to marry someone who accepts Christ in the same way you do. Since faith is a vital part of life, you need to share your life with a person who feels the same way. Otherwise you could have a terrible time trying to keep your faith fresh, alive, and real.

We all want to be open-minded and tolerant of other religions. We respect people even if we don't agree with them. But when it comes to marriage, it is too risky to become partners with a spouse who rejects the Christ who is at the center of our lives.

It isn't too early to begin to pray for God's guidance in finding the person you will marry. Ask for the wisdom to pick out a special someone who has faith in Jesus Christ.

The question isn't whether the person is Protestant, Jewish, Catholic, Muslim, Buddhist, or Hindu. The issue is Jesus Christ. It is tremendously difficult to serve and worship the Son of God if your partner does not. And it's difficult to have a deep friend-ship with a spouse who does not share the same faith.

> Do not be yoked together with unbelievers.
> *2 Corinthians 6:14*

Think It Over

1. What are three of the more important qualities you want in a husband or wife?
2. Would you like God's guidance in selecting a mate?
3. Have you begun to pray that God will help you in the process?

Why Have Devotions?

Apparently most teenagers have devotions for one or more of the following reasons.

1. They get revved up at youth group or at camp and decide to read the Bible and pray daily.
2. They feel guilty about something and decide they had better get close to God.
3. They feel good about God and want to communicate with him.

These aren't the only reasons, but they seem to be the major ones. Each of these could be a good reason to get started, but naturally, the third seems like the best.

There is no biblical law that says we *must* read the Bible and pray every day. Communication with God happens in many ways at different times and under a wide array of circumstances.

Instead of rules on how to talk to God, we should be looking for guidelines. What would be helpful? Are there certain ways that make it easier? What are the benefits of keeping in close contact? Is God like a friend that we love to keep in touch with, only a whole lot more?

Don't be surprised if you find that you read and pray regularly for a few days or a few weeks and then quit. Later you may start again and do it for a short while again. Discipline isn't easy for most of us. Don't feel like a prune pit just because you have trouble being consistent.

Visiting with God can be an attractive proposition. There are many good, compelling reasons to stay in close communication. Don't be frightened off by tons of laws on how to do it.

Today it may be great to pray one way. Tomorrow the time and place might change. The third day it might not happen at all. On the fourth day you could be praying at a bungee jump.

Try not to get bogged down in the details. Be loose. Be open. Be willing. Be transparent. Be pliable. Be fresh. Be real. Be sincere. It's more exciting to visit with a friend if we can be that way.

After leaving them, he went up on a mountainside to pray.

Mark 6:46

Think It Over

1. Where is your favorite place to talk to God?
2. When is your favorite time to talk to God?
3. What do you get or experience from visiting with God?

A Turtle Goes to Norway

If you read the story in the paper, you must have wondered when the turtle first knew it was in trouble. Giant turtles that live near Mexico don't usually swim in the cold waters of Norway.

The seven-and-a-half-foot, 730-pound turtle was probably wandering around in the Gulf Stream looking for something to do. Life had become boring, munching on the same old fish, sniffing slimy algae all day long. Slowly, aimlessly the lazy leatherback pushed off into new waterways and eventually found itself far from home.

When a fishing trawler lifted its net near the Arctic Circle, the fishermen were startled to find this tremendous turtle tangled inside. The reptile had roamed 8,000 miles across the ocean to a place where it clearly didn't belong.

Fortunately, the monstrous turtle was given a safe air flight back to Mexico where it could pick up its life again in warmer waters.

How many times have we sensed that we were wandering away, but we didn't do anything about it? Inch by inch, day by day, we knew that we were swimming farther and farther out. We were leaving our base, our beliefs, our commitments, our values, our relationship to Jesus Christ.

Some people take a big leap and leave everything they count important, but most of us don't do it that way. More often we go a little farther each day, and eventually we no longer know how to get back.

At some point the turtle knew something was wrong. The water kept getting colder. The food didn't taste as good. The days

90

were shorter. It didn't see any of the old familiar reptiles any-more. But the turtle either couldn't or wouldn't turn around.

At some time all of us know we ought to turn around. We are with the wrong crowd, we are trying the wrong substance, we are in the wrong place. We are drifting farther and farther away, and we need to do something about it. Sometimes we do, and sometimes we don't.

This is a good day to check your bearings. Are you going too far with something? Too far with someone? Too far from what really counts? Too far from God?

Not everybody gets a safe, free ride back on an airplane. You may need to turn around today before you go too far. It would be easy to just drift away.

We must pay more careful attention, therefore, to what we have heard, so that we do not drift away.

Hebrews 2:1

Think It Over

1. Have you started to do something that you wish you weren't doing?
2. Why don't you stop doing it?
3. Will you take a big step today and stop drifting?
4. What will that step be?

Feeling Ugly

Have you ever watched a potter while he or she works the clay? It looks like a blob of mud. The potter dumps it on the flat wheel, adds water and starts spinning. As the clay spins, the potter digs into it with his or her fingers, working, molding, shaping the work.

There is a very famous singer today who as a child saw himself as ugly, complete with large ears and eyes like saucers. The grandson of a minister, he would pray that people would think he was funny, so he would have some purpose in life.

The Great Potter wasn't done shaping the young man. Now as a young adult he regularly performs in front of tens of thousands who come to see him in concert. On television his fans can be counted in the millions.

Each of us is a piece of clay. Our heavenly Potter continues to work on us, molding us into something new. He works on us when we are six and is still working when we are sixty.

Our heavenly Potter is busy shaping more than just the outside of the pottery. Inside, he wants to make us complete, loving, sharing, and spiritual. Sometimes we don't want to be worked on. We want to be left alone. At other times we want to be the loveliest, most ornate, extra-special piece of pottery that ever existed. But God knows what kind of pottery he wants us to be.

God doesn't want us all to be singers, or boat captains, or airline pilots. He molds and shapes each of us for different purposes. Each day, each week, each year we are changed, improved, and refined by the Master Potter.

Smart people become happy with the work God is doing. They become grateful for who they are and what they are becoming. Relax and let the Potter work his art.

Like clay in the hand of the potter, so are you in my hand.
Jeremiah 18:6

Think It Over

1. Do you feel down about your appearance and abilities?
2. How do you resist the temptation to get down on yourself?
3. Do you trust God to keep working on you?

What in the World Is Worship?

I looked up the word worship, and this is what I learned. It comes from an old English word that means "worthship" or worthiness. When we worship, we are acknowledging the fact that God is worthy to receive our devotion, our service, our dedication, and a lot of other good things.

We have a wide range of ways to worship.

Some of us bow down in church.
Some of us sing songs of praise.
Some of us give money.
Some of us take communion.
Some of us do all of that and more.

In some form we are agreeing that God is worthy of our allegiance, our respect, and our love.

Church isn't the only place where we worship. You might bow your head at home, give praise to God in your bedroom, or sing to God in your small group.

Often we worship God by our activities. We might feed the hungry, teach a child, tell Bible stories, or help the homeless. When we do that as a service to God, we are worshiping him.

If we sacrifice something for the service of God, that is also a form of worship. We give money away, share our clothing, or take food to the poor, and we do it as a sacrifice to God. We are worshiping the King.

There are countless ways to worship God. Anything we do because we are in submission to God, anything we do to bring glory to his name, anything we do that admits he is in charge can be an act of worship.

And worship can be great for the person who worships. By kneeling, working, singing, and sacrificing we get our eyes off ourselves. We put our attention on God and those he wants us to serve.

It's a cool idea. Worship puts life in perfect order.

Yet a time is coming and has now come when the true worshipers will worship the Father in spirit and truth, for they are the kind of worshipers the Father seeks. God is spirit, and his worshipers must worship in spirit and in truth.

John 4:23–24

Think It Over

1. What are two of your favorite ways to worship?
2. Do you sometimes worship God by yourself?
3. Have you sacrificed anything for God lately?

Book Covers

Looking for a good project? Do you belong to a youth group that wants to try something exciting? Have you thought about book covers with smart messages on them? Good, positive phrases like:

Accept one another.
Bad company corrupts good character.
Do everything in love.
Be a person of courage.
Do not repay anyone evil for evil.
Do not steal.
Love does no harm to its neighbor.
Forgive as the Lord forgave you.
Do not get drunk.

Teens receive so many negative messages that a few positive ones could help. Talk to your friends about which phrases to use and the colors to select. You'll need to raise a few bucks for the printing.

A group at a high school in the Midwest had thousands of book covers printed and distributed to anyone who wanted them. Naturally some teens laughed at the messages, but others appreciated the encouragement. They might help change the tone around school just a little.

It isn't that people haven't heard the quotes before. The problem is that negative messages crowd out the positive ones.

Part of the Christian message should be that it's all right to think straight.

Talk it over and see what comes of the idea.

Keep reminding them of these things.
2 Timothy 2:14

Think It Over

1. Decide who should discuss the project.
2. How could you make the project better?
3. Can you picture God using a venture like this?

Wild Living

Lowell Thomas, a famous journalist and traveler, described himself as an explorer and not an adventurer. An explorer wants new experiences. He wants to see a wide variety of places and cultures. An adventurer takes unnecessary chances and could easily get hurt.

Young people often want to explore and learn new things. They want to get out and sample life instead of sitting in their rooms counting flowers on the wallpaper. That's normal.

Unfortunately some teenagers insist on adventure. They want to take risks. Drinking and driving, trying drugs, and running away are all part of the menu.

Not long ago a couple of sixteen-year-old boys were offered a substance called jimsonweed. Their "reliable" friends told them it couldn't hurt anyone. The boys tried some, then each of them went to their homes. Later, they began to have hallucinations. One boy believed things were coming out of his closet.

Their parents rushed them to the hospital, but the doctors couldn't figure out what the teens had taken. The boys had trouble breathing, and both were afraid they might die. Finally the doctors were able to help, and they survived.

It makes sense to sample the good parts of life. But it's dumb to think you have to try the dangerous ones. That's one of the reasons that the Lord puts certain stop signs along the road. There are some things that are too threatening, too foolish, and too harmful to mess with. God isn't trying to kill our fun, but he is interested in protecting us from "things coming out of the closet."

The story of the prodigal son tells us that the young man took his share of the inheritance and went out and spent it on "wild living." He wanted to experiment, try things, take chances. In the end he was broke, embarrassed, and nearly starved to death.

Eventually he returned home and was lovingly accepted by his father.

Explore life. Sample the good things. But stay away from the things that hurt people.

> Not long after that, the younger son got together all he had, set off for a distant country and there squandered his wealth in wild living.

Luke 15:13

Think It Over

1. Why do people try drugs?
2. Do you have to try "everything"?
3. Why does God warn us about wild living?

The Sacrifice of Fools

Have you ever wanted something so much that you would do almost anything to get it? Did you ever want a boyfriend, a career, a lead in the play, or a car so much that it hurt to even think about it?

Sometimes when we wish too hard, we make foolish promises to God.

> "Lord, if you let me become a cheerleader, I promise to always follow you."
> "All I ever want is to become an airline flight attendant. Make me one of those and I'll give you 20 percent of my income. Honest, Lord."
> "I just have to have a new cassette player. Lord, give me one, and I'll work at the soup kitchen every Saturday for a year."
> "Lord, if you get me out of trouble with the law, I promise to join the church. I'll do it right away."
> "Lord, if you bring me safely through surgery, I promise I'll become a missionary to any place you want."

The Lord understands promises that are made under pressure. He doesn't expect us to keep a deal that we made in a foolish moment.

In Ecclesiastes 5:1–7 the author calls these the sacrifices of fools. The author is often blunt and sometimes rude. But he gets the point across.

Don't feel that you have to follow through with a dumb promise that was made in haste to God. The Lord doesn't hold us to words we never should have said.

Too many of us feel guilty because we promised too much. God will let you off the hook. Some young people try to become missionaries because of a vow they made during a lightning storm when they were nine years old.

God is interested in commitments, but only real ones. He wants us to keep the promises we made because we love him. The Lord isn't worried about the vows we made in order to get a new bike.

The sacrifices of fools don't really count, but God appreciates promises from the heart.

> Guard your steps when you go to the house of God. Go near to listen rather than to offer the sacrifice of fools, who do not know that they do wrong. Do not be quick with your mouth, do not be hasty in your heart to utter anything before God.
>
> *Ecclesiastes 5:1–2*

Think It Over

1. Have you ever tried to cut a foolish deal with God?
2. Did you try to keep the promise?
3. Have you ever sacrificed anything to God without making a deal?

First Reactions

Don't think these over. Simply read down the list and give your first reaction to each statement.

Women aren't as smart as men.
Men are insensitive.
Black people are lazy.
Lawyers are obnoxious.
Jews are greedy.
Hispanics are dumb.
Smart kids are nerds.
Blondes are dumb.
Teenagers are irresponsible.
Gays have AIDS.
TV ministers are crooks.
Teachers are mean.
Overweight people are lazy.
Whites are selfish.

We better quit because it's getting too long. Each item on the list is a prejudice. There are ways we prejudge people, and we don't even know we're doing it.

Every person is different. God doesn't want us to judge people we have never met. Christians need to back off and stop being so prejudiced.

Then Peter began to speak: "I now realize how true it is that God does not show favoritism."

Acts 10:34

104

Think It Over

1. Are there people who are prejudiced against you? How do you handle it?
2. Are you a friend to people who are different?
3. Have you ever asked God to help make you more accepting to all kinds of people?

God's Mysterious Will

It's hard to see the big picture. Most of us want answers to the great questions of life.

Does God want you to be the president of IBM?
Should you apply for dental school?
Does God want you as a missionary?
Should you marry the town butcher?
Does God want you to become an aquanaut?
Does God want you rich?
Should you become a race car driver?

Those are all worthwhile decisions that you might need to make. As you start to put the puzzle together, it's hard to discover exactly how God wants to work in your life.

Maybe it's too tough to try to figure out the big ones. You may have to back up and ask God to give you direction in the little decisions.

For instance, God tells you his will very plainly in some sections of the Bible. He tells you that it's his will that you be thankful. That's direct, plain, uncluttered. But many of us ignore this small piece of his will and remain grouchy.

If you want to follow the will of God, you need to obey the small parts first. What is God's will for you today, right now, precisely where you live? His will is that you drop your sourpuss face, change your grumpy attitude, stop complaining, and become thankful.

But that isn't what you were looking for. You wanted to hear about the big picture. Does God want you in the mountains of Tibet?

106

Hold on. Back up. What about God's will one brick at a time? You need to work on thankfulness before you reach out to bigger things.

If God says his will is for you to be thankful, how wise is it to keep an attitude?

Be joyful always; pray continually; give thanks in all circumstances, for this is God's will for you in Christ Jesus.
1 Thessalonians 5:16–18

Think It Over

1. Are you interested in God's guidance for this day?
2. Would you like to have his attitude?
3. Can you ask the Lord to make you more thankful?

A Book We Can Trust

In a recent survey 85 percent of the teenagers who were asked said they believed the Bible was the inspired word of God. Doesn't that amaze you? With so many individuals, teachers, writers, and articles knocking the Bible, it's surprising that so many young people hold it in such high regard.

Teenagers often have a far greater faith than adults realize. Young people frequently want God to be part of their lives and watch over them. Those same teens look for ways to serve God and help others.

It would be easy for a young person to think he or she is alone in his or her faith. That isn't the case. Many teens are uncomfortable expressing their beliefs. They aren't sure how to put them into words. But in their hearts they are willing and eager to trust in Jesus Christ.

Millions of young people attend some kind of Bible study regularly. They wear crosses. They own religious plaques. Teens may not feel comfortable about showing their faith the same way adults do, but their faith is often there. Many feel out of place in church, but that doesn't mean Christ isn't real to them.

It's harder to believe and follow Christ if you think no one else does. We could keep our faith if we were the only Christians at school, but it would be more difficult.

Believers are not a fading group. Many who have made no commitment to Christ still believe the Bible is the Word of God. We aren't in the minority, as some would have us think. If we were in the minority, we would still follow Christ; but the fact is, we aren't.

Be encouraged! Many believers do not stand up for Christ as they should. Some Christians have never had good teaching in the Scriptures. But, down deep, they do believe.

All Scripture is God-breathed and is useful for teaching, rebuking, correcting and training in righteousness.

2 Timothy 3:16

Think It Over

1. When you read the Bible, do you expect to learn from God?
2. Do you have a favorite part of the Bible that you like to read?
3. When do you enjoy reading the Bible the most?

Bumper Sticker Wisdom

How many of us get guidance for our lives by reading bumper stickers? We used to break open fortune cookies to find words of wisdom, but now all we have to do is pull up to a red light and get a thought for today.

Be careful which ones you read. One will insult you and say you are driving too close. The next one will tell you his wife rides a broomstick. A third sticker will tell you to ride the Stomach Plunger at Bob's Amusement Park.

One of the sternest, harshest stickers is the one that teaches "Don't Get Mad—Get Even." It's such an unpleasant thought that I am startled almost every time I see it. I suppose that its real purpose is to shock people.

The fact is, this sticker expresses what many of us think. If someone

    insults us,
    hurts us,
    cheats us,
    ignores us,
    forgets us,
    ridicules us,

we feel we need to get even.

This is one of the big reasons that so many people are picking up weapons and blowing each other away. They are looking for a way to get even, plus do a little more damage.

Armed gunmen are walking into offices, restaurants, schools, law firms, and court rooms and blazing away. What makes people do that? Too many are trying to get even because of some wrong they feel has been done to them.

Their moral mathematics are wrong. They believe that if they are wronged, they must do someone else a wrong in return. Often they do several people wrong, as if they deserve a bonus.

Christian morals teach us to do the opposite. We learn to:

Love our enemies.
Forgive those who trespass against us.
Turn the other cheek.
Bless those that curse us.

Maybe we need a Christian bumper sticker that says, "Don't Get Mad—Forgive Them."

Do not take revenge, my friends, but leave room for God's wrath, for it is written: "It is mine to avenge, I will repay."

Romans 12:19

Think It Over

1. When someone does you wrong, do you have a strong urge to get him back?
2. What do you do with that urge?
3. Have you ever decided not to get even and simply turn the matter over to God?

Matt Had HIV

When Matt was thirteen years old, he announced that he had HIV. A hemophiliac, he had contracted the virus through a transfusion. It must have been difficult to go public, especially since he couldn't be sure how people would react to him.

For the next four years Matt was a great example of courage and happiness. His friends said he lived life to its fullest. A local pastor said the teen held no resentment or bitterness.

Matt spoke at elementary schools, high schools, colleges, and civic groups. He was vice-president of his senior class, band president, honor society member, and more. When he died, hundreds packed into the high school gymnasium to say good-bye to the seventeen-year-old.

If Matt had become bitter over his bad break, we would have understood. None of us likes to get hurt or to have a rotten deal. Some of us have become bitter over little things. Imagine if we ever received a terrible blow like this one.

Bitterness is much like strangling slowly. We keep choking and choking over some problem we have.

It would be easy to get bitter.

We weigh too much.
Our hair is stringy.
Our parents are divorced.
We have an illness.
We weigh too little.
Our brother is a dropout.
We're broke.
We can't get a date.

We flunked history.
Our grandfather is terribly sick.
Our home flooded.
We didn't make the team.

All of us have a list (maybe a long list) of things that hurt. The temptation to become bitter and sour is really strong.

The Bible simply tells us not to do it. Bitterness is something we can control. We aren't helpless. I had a friend who had had a bad foot since birth. When I knew him, he was a teenager who was active in everything. He didn't make room for bitterness. He was too busy involving himself in life.

There are no magic formulas here. We can't count on a friend to take our bitterness away. We have to make a conscious decision to chase it away and take a big bite out of life.

> Get rid of all bitterness, rage and anger, brawling and slander, along with every form of malice.
>
> *Ephesians 4:31*

Think It Over

1. Can you think of one thing that most often gets you down?
2. How do you stop feeling sorry for yourself and begin living?
3. Tell God you are tired of being bitter, and tell him what you intend to do about it.

A $92,000 Gorilla

There was a man who had a great deal of money. No one said where he got it, but he had a bunch. This man wanted to use the money to buy a gorilla. What's wrong with that? Maybe he just happened to like big monkeys.

His plan was to buy the gorilla and smuggle it back to his country. That was the problem: It was illegal to take a gorilla to his homeland.

The police discovered that the man was looking for an illegal animal. They decided to put a special agent in a gorilla's suit to pretend to be a gorilla. The ploy worked. The man paid $92,000 for a phony gorilla and had it shipped to his country.

When the human gorilla arrived, the police arrested the purchaser for breaking the law. The man they arrested knew primates, and he had a bundle of money; but he still bought a person in a gorilla suit.

As one person who watched it all said, "He fell for it. It goes to show you money doesn't mean somebody is intelligent."

All of us are capable of acting like fools. We may never buy a phony gorilla, but we may do something just as foolish. We waste our money on dumb parties, we gamble it away, or we buy gadgets that barely work. We've all done it.

I knew a young man who saved hundreds of dollars for college but shot it all in one weekend in Baltimore. I know a teen who bought a junker car and was always broke trying to keep the piece of trash rolling.

Most of us learn after the first time or two. But too many of us don't learn until the sixth or seventh time. Some of us are

114

slow learners in financial matters, and we lose a great deal before it sinks in.

Don't be too proud to ask your parents for advice. They may recognize a phony gorilla when they see one. We usually survive the financial dumb-dumbs, but it's a hard way to learn. If it keeps happening, be quick to talk to your parents.

Of what use is money in the hand of a fool, since he has no desire to get wisdom?

Proverbs 17:16

Think It Over

1. Have you ever wasted money on a "gorilla"? What was it?
2. Have you ever bought anything sold on TV or in a magazine and lived to regret it?
3. Whom would you go to if you had a financial question?

Give Yourself a Hand

Some days we think we're pretty hot stuff—

> just a little better than someone else,
> a tad more important,
> maybe a smidgen more valuable—than others.

It's a common feeling. Most of us start to think we are more than special.

> Possibly a bit extra special,
> a notch beyond confident,
> the pick of the litter.

And once in a while we think that no one else is quite as good as we are. That we are

> easier to get along with,
> more clever and funnier,
> and have better insights
> than those around us.

We become so full of ourselves that we begin to bubble over. Soon it isn't enough to think we are better. We even start saying we are better than others.

> We start to brag.
> We begin to boast.
> We talk about ourselves.
> More and more.

The Bible tells us that when we begin to brag too much about how great we are that we also should give ourselves a hand—and that hand should go right over our mouth.

If you have played the fool and exalted yourself, or if you have planned evil, clap your hand over your mouth!

Proverbs 30:32

Think It Over

1. Do you ever feel you are better than someone who doesn't get grades as good as yours?
2. Do you ever talk about yourself in order to make someone else feel bad?
3. Ask God to make you feel confident without feeling cocky.

Lock 'Em Up!

Is there a gun in your house that is not locked up? Would you ask your parents to please put it safely away? Ask them to put the weapon in one place and the ammunition in another. Too many teens are shooting people, and gun safety might cut down on that number.

Stories similar to the following have appeared in many big city newspapers.

> A thirteen-year-old boy got pushed around. One day a group of white boys roughed him up. On another day a group of African-Americans drove past him on the street and threatened him. Frightened and intimidated, the teenager took his father's loaded gun to school to defend himself.

The number of shootings among young people has grown enormously. Teens are being sentenced to twenty to thirty years or even life because they get a gun and use it to deal with their problems. Because students often bring guns to school, the authorities are forced to regularly search students and lockers, trying to keep the problem under control.

What can one teen do to help? Why not deal with the situation where you live? You can't imagine ever picking up a gun and going after another teen. The thirteen-year-old probably couldn't imagine it either. In one case, a teen, visiting at another house, became angry, grabbed a loaded pistol off the refrigerator, and killed another teen. We all need to become more aware of what can happen when there are guns around.

Help your parents help you. Tell them your concern. The avail-
ability of the gun and bullets in your home makes the setting too
dangerous.

God has always been concerned about the violence among his
people. We are told about violent acts as early as Cain and Abel
in Genesis 4. The Bible is concerned about the unfaithful who
have a craving for violence (Proverbs 13:2).

We may not be able to stop violence, but maybe we can put a
small dent in it. Why not take the first step at home?

As for the deeds of men—by the words of your lips I have
kept myself from the ways of the violent.

Psalm 17:4

Think It Over

1. What could you and your parents do to make your house
   a safe zone?
2. What can the Christians at school do to reduce anger and
   hostility?
3. Ask your youth group to brainstorm some ways that God
   might want you to bring about local peace.

A Bum Relationship

Think hard and be very honest with yourself.

Do you have a relationship with a male or a female that isn't good for you? Are you friends with someone who is hurting you physically, emotionally, or spiritually?

Most of us would have trouble admitting that we are in a bad relationship. Sometimes we are even attracted to people who do us harm.

There must be millions of silent sufferers everywhere. One report claims that 30 to 40 percent of teenage girls have been hit on a date. Do you wonder how many of those went on a second date with this same abuser?

Some teenagers think it's normal to be yelled at, called names, degraded, or smacked. They may have grown up in homes where they were abused, and they think everyone does it.

Everyone doesn't hit. Friends hitting friends is not normal—nor is it good. Physical violence, verbal violence, and sexual violence are terrible, and should never be tolerated. No one should remain in a relationship where he or she is being mistreated.

Too many young people believe that they deserve to be abused. They think they are worthless and shouldn't expect anything better. That's wrong. None of us deserve to be mistreated.

If you feel confused and wonder about your relationship, tell someone how you feel. Tell another friend, a parent, a counselor, a minister. Ask them to listen while you describe your situation. Let them react to what is going on in your life.

No teenager should stay in a harmful friendship. God didn't create us to be degraded by someone else. Ask God for the courage to stand up, step out, and do something about that bum relationship.

> A righteous man is cautious in friendship.
> *Proverbs 12:26*

Think It Over

1. Do you have a friend who has hit you? Why do you stay friends?
2. Is there a friend who makes you feel useless, dumb, unattractive, or cheap? Why do you stay friends?
3. Name a friend who makes you feel great about yourself.

Television Crazies

Recently one of my television sets stopped working, so I took it to the shop. They spent a couple of weeks repairing it. While the set was gone, a true American tragedy happened: My second set quit. Try to imagine the trauma. Think of the terror. I had to spend hours at home without a talking box to occupy my little brain and amuse me.

Before long I had to resort to reading so I wouldn't develop a nervous twitch. I read about Sweden, the Amazon, and Tibet. Rusty at first, I soon saw a few of my reading skills begin to kick in again.

It's amazing how dependent we are on television. TV viewing must be right up there with chocolate, pizza, and soft drinks as some of life's essential ingredients. The ideal life seems to be watching television while we eat. The majority of us mix these two together regularly.

Not many of us like to admit we watch a great deal of television. "Oh, I hardly watch any at all," we insist. But ask about shows and stars, and we know them all.

Let's not go on a tirade against TV. Television has its place and actually can be very helpful. Good comedy, good news, good mysteries, good sports, good nature—how can you beat it? There are also some crummy things on, so we have to choose.

The most important question is whether or not you do anything besides watch TV. Do you read anything? Do you have conversations with family and friends? Do you have a hobby? Do you belong to a group or two?

When do you meditate? When do you think? When do you talk to God? When do you sit alone and ask God to bring thoughts to your mind?

Most of us aren't very good at spending hours with God, but even a few minutes will help. Steal a little time away from the tube and get to know God better.

> But his delight is in the law of the LORD, and on his law he meditates day and night.
>
> *Psalm 1:2*

Think It Over

1. Are you emotionally addicted to TV?
2. Is the TV on all the time?
3. When do you visit alone with the Lord?

Can't Please Everybody!

A young teen stood in a courtroom waiting to hear the judge give her sentence. Her crime was breaking into a convenience store late at night and robbing it. That's what the state believed her crime to be. Actually this youth committed a more basic crime than that. She was a girl who wanted to please everybody.

When a friend said, "Come on, we'll have a good time; besides nobody gets caught," this teen didn't want to disappoint anyone. So she went along.

Adults often think teens don't want to please anyone, but the fact is that many young people try to please all of their friends. They are pleasers by personality. They think that if they do almost everything their friends want, their friends will like them.

They want acceptance.
They want approval.
They want to be included.
They want to be invited.
They want to be wanted.

All of these feelings are good and normal. Not many of us want to be excluded and ignored.

The real question is what do we have to pay in order to gain acceptance?

How far do we have to go?
What price will we pay?
Which compromises do we make?
How much do we reduce our values?

Often very good people do some very bad things. All they were trying to do was please somebody, and the results were disastrous.

Hold back. Don't be so willing and so foolish to please. It's far more important to please God than to get out of joint trying to please people.

Be kind, thoughtful, and caring. But keep the lines clearly drawn, and refuse to go too far.

Am I now trying to win the approval of men, or of God? Or am I trying to please men? If I were still trying to please men, I would not be a servant of Christ.

Galatians 1:10

Think It Over

1. Have you ever done something stupid trying to please your friends?
2. Are you a "pleaser" who tries to make everybody happy?
3. Is it important for you to try to please God?

Getting Pregnant

No sermons here. No advice. No heart-wrenching lectures. Many teenagers seem untouched by the appeals given by adults. Instead, let's list the facts, and you weigh them for yourself.

Most teenagers who get pregnant end up being single parents.
Most teens probably say, "It won't happen to me."
People who become single parents usually live in poverty.
Someone said, "If you become pregnant as a teen, most of your major decisions in life have been made for you."
The great majority of fathers who should pay child support never pay.
Despite the promises made by men, most pregnant teens do not marry.
In the overwhelming majority of cases, she takes care of the baby, not him.
A higher percentage of babies born to teenagers have physical and mental problems.

Many of the young people I know hate these arguments. They shrug off the facts. They think the odds are very small that pregnancy will happen.

But someone has to say it. (Maybe one teen will read this and think again.) Premarital sex has consequences, and many of those consequences last a lifetime.

Ask the Lord to give you wisdom. It takes a lot of wisdom to deal with something as beautiful as sex.

If any of you lacks wisdom, he should ask God, who gives generously to all without finding fault, and it will be given to him.

James 1:5

(P.S. If you insist on ignoring these facts, please use protection.)

Think It Over

1. How would your life change if you or your date got pregnant?
2. What is the best guarantee that it won't happen?
3. If you don't want to listen to an adult about pregnancy, whom would you listen to?

Teenage Vampires

It sounds like a low-grade movie, but it really does happen. There are some teens who have turned to drinking blood. Evidently their lives were so empty and meaningless that they experimented at being vampires.

A group of teenagers in Texas were getting together and biting each other in the back. Then they sucked blood as if they were in a horror movie. For at least six months half a dozen teens had been meeting in search of special gifts and deliverance from problems. Then an older teenager convinced the group that acting like vampires would give them extra powers.

This continued until the parents of one of the teens worried about the bite marks on their daughter's back. Eventually they went to the police. More than simply a prank or dare, the participants actually persuaded themselves that they were vampires. They wanted to play with satanic power.

These forms of satanic practices may not be very widespread. They get a great deal of publicity, and they are interesting, but they aren't sweeping the country at this point.

What should concern everyone is the desperate need we all have to find purpose in life. Too many people of all ages have no reason to live. If we feel unwanted, unloved, and disconnected, we might get into all kinds of bizarre activities.

Blood slurping doesn't sound attractive to most of us, but empty people may try almost anything. Many teens using drugs, alcohol, sex, thrills, and danger simply don't know what else to do with themselves. If you feel like you have no reason to get up in the morning, you might try something dangerous too.

Teens who accept Jesus Christ as their Savior have real purpose in life. They don't have to chase after cheap kicks to find
something to do.

God wants all of us to be part of him. He picks us up and wants
to give us a good reason to live. Following Jesus Christ gives us
goals and meaning in this world.

In him we were also chosen, having been predestined
according to the plan of him who works out everything in
conformity with the purpose of his will.

Ephesians 1:11

Think It Over

1. Do you consider yourself a follower of Jesus Christ?
2. Have you invited Christ into your life?
3. Are you trying to serve Christ?

Time to Defuse

We've all heard stories about it. Someone has a problem that's hard to handle. He doesn't do anything about it, and eventually it builds up inside. One day, unexpectedly, he blows up and does something terrible.

The newspaper had a story about a fifteen-year-old boy who was pushed around for years by a large sixteen-year-old boy at school. The article said the big boy was mean. Not only did he tease the smaller teen, but he hit and shoved him around.

Unable to deal with the abuse any longer, the fifteen-year-old brought a handgun to school in his book bag. During geology class he walked over to the bully and shot him twice at point-blank range, killing him.

How could the situation have been prevented? Wasn't there someone he could have talked to? Could a transfer have been arranged? Could a teacher have spoken bluntly to the bully?

All of us face mounting pressure from time to time. A problem gets in our way and begins to grow larger and larger.

Schoolwork gets too tough.
A friend treats us terribly.
We don't have the right clothes.
We get left out of a party.
Our parents become impossible.

Whatever the pressure, it gets too big to handle all alone. Before the problem grows too large, it's important to talk to two people: another person and God.

Talk to an adult, a parent, or a friend your age. Tell him or her what is bothering you and why. You will feel better if you can say it—and maybe the person can make some suggestions.

Talk to God and tell him what's going on. Again, you will feel better for saying it, and God may change something. He may change the problem or he could change your outlook on the problem.

If you take the fuse out of the dynamite, you defuse the explosive. Take the fuse out of your problem by discussing it with someone you respect.

Is any one of you in trouble? He should pray.
James 5:13

Think It Over

1. Are you having trouble sleeping because of a problem?
2. Are you thinking about getting even with someone?
3. Is there someone you could talk to today about your problem?

Moshers Riding High

Have you ever gone moshing?

Moshing is a sport that thousands of young people have learned to play. It's sort of like surfing on a sea of people.

A crowd of young people at a concert or a beach party pick someone up, and the moshing begins. The person is hoisted into the air on one foot. Then he or she lays back and is passed along over the crowd. Those who have tried it say the best way is to keep your body rigid. A relaxed person is harder to pass over the crowd.

A mosher has to trust the moshing crowd. You have to believe that the people will not suddenly stop and let you fall to the floor. You also have to believe that the teens will be strong enough to hold you up. If you get passed into a section of six people who are only half trying, you can go plummeting downward.

When the ride is over, you might yell, "I want off," but it's tricky. If the group doesn't let you down gently, you could get a terrible lump on your head.

It's hard to trust in people, especially strangers. Have you ever played the game where someone falls backwards into the arms of six waiting friends? It takes a lot of trust to let go and expect someone to come through for you.

God hasn't invited us to go moshing or to fall backwards, but he does encourage us to trust him. Sometimes we need to lay back and believe that God will come through and hold us up.

We can think of reasons not to do that. What if God decides to drop us? What if we look foolish depending on God? What if God carries us in a direction we don't want to go? Moshing with

God isn't easy. It can even be scary. But often moshing is the best way to count on God.

When we feel out of control, when we feel like we're losing, when we feel like our world is falling apart, that's when it is especially important to fall back and rest in the hands of a Lord who cares about us.

And the one who trusts in him will never be put to shame.

1 Peter 2:6

Think It Over

1. Name three people you really trust.
2. Can people trust or depend on you?
3. Do you ever commit the night or the day to the Lord and trust him to take care of it?

135

Adopt a Kid

Once a week Lisa looks up the kid she has "adopted." She spends time with Casey. They get a soft drink together and go over his homework. Casey is in the fifth grade, and he loves the attention he gets from this high school junior.

Casey was restless in school. His home life was a little shaky. He needed both a tutor and an older friend.

Their relationship might last for only a few months or a year. Maybe it will last longer, but for a while Casey will have a special person in his life. He probably thinks a junior in high school is mature and neat, and he enjoys being around her.

There are many Caseys in our neighborhoods and schools. They need an extra break. They need someone to reach out and give them loads of encouragement.

One year our church had a program designed to do this. For almost a year I was able to go weekly to a local restaurant with a young teen, and we visited together. I learned a great deal from him, and I will always remember those as days filled with meaning.

It takes courage to start a relationship like this, but it can be done. Some teens do it by themselves, while others get organized and get involved as a group. One night of tutoring at church would allow teens to have a tremendous influence on grade school kids.

Jesus put a heavy emphasis on the importance of one person. He talked about the shepherd who leaves his ninety-nine sheep in order to go and find the one sheep who has wandered away. We seem to put a lot of energy into programs and events, and too often we ignore the one person.

Pause. Look around. Ask the Lord to fill your heart with compassion for a single individual. As the Holy Spirit molds the way you think, you might find someone to help for a few months, maybe a year. Let Christ be seen in you by the way you care for others.

Suppose one of you has a hundred sheep and loses one of them. Does he not leave the ninety-nine in the open country and go after the lost sheep until he finds it?

Luke 15:4

Think It Over

1. Is this the kind of thing you would like to do?
2. Can you think of an older person who was special to you?
3. Would you like to ask the Lord to make you alert to a kid you might be able to help?

Calling Psychics

They seem to be everywhere. Ads on television, columns in newspapers, books on the shelves, and of course 900 telephone numbers. Psychics, palm readers, and astrologers are just a few of the people who are waiting to tell your future and make predictions.

Even famous people like movie stars, actors, and political figures say that psychics have helped them. Reportedly, they have found love, fortunes, and careers from consulting their psychics.

These kinds of people have a great appeal because they promise help. All of us would like help; so we are drawn to them, and we want to believe they're for real.

One of the things that seems strange is that at the bottom of the television ad for psychics there is a note explaining that the phone call is for entertainment only. That doesn't sound like they are willing to back up their predictions.

Psychics aren't new. They have been around in some form for centuries. But do they have special power to see the future? Probably not; maybe some of them do have the ability to see tomorrow. Maybe there are people around who are able to get a glimpse of the future. But even if there is a trace of truth to this power, it's important to know that not all power is good. Does this insight come from godly sources or evil sources?

There probably is no legitimacy to psychics, but what if there is a little?

The Bible doesn't argue over what diviners or psychics can or can't do, and it doesn't tell us to try them. The Bible simply tells us to stay away from the people who do this.

All that I have seen of this practice is a joke. The 900 phone calls and the newspaper predictions seem silly to me. But there could be unusual forces at work in some people.

Keep these thoughts in mind:

1. You could get some terrible advice.
2. You might waste a lot of money.
3. You could get more involved than you intend.
4. You could be pulled away from Christ.
5. The Bible tells us to have nothing to do with psychics.

Most of us like to dabble in the mysterious and the titillating. We also want to be told that something great is going to come our way. But getting involved in the wrong things could become very painful.

The Bible calls it divination, the ability to figure out the future. God has told us to stay away from those who say they can do this.

> The nations you will dispossess listen to those who practice sorcery or divination. But as for you, the Lord your God has not permitted you to do so.
> *Deuteronomy 18:14*

Think It Over

1. Do you feel good about trusting God for tomorrow?
2. Can you take one day at a time and enjoy each day?
3. Can you commit tomorrow to the Lord and face the day with him?

Confession

Do you have a burden that
   you're tired of carrying around?
Would you like to get some relief
   by getting it off your shoulders?

Why not tell the Lord what the problem is and lighten your load? Why not be honest, up-front, and frank about what's bothering you?

The Lord will not chew you out, condemn you, or make you feel like dirt. He will understand, love, and forgive you.

No matter what the problem is.

God is shockproof. He has heard confessions about murder, stealing, sex, hate, abuse, and all sorts of mean activities. He has forgiven all of these and more.

Only you know what is bothering you. Maybe you need to talk to a professional counselor, but maybe not. One good plan is to start by talking with God.

Most of us carry secrets around. When I was young, I did something I was ashamed of. But God has forgiven me, and I no longer haul the shame on my shoulders. God listened to my confession and still loves me.

Maybe you are carrying a secret. It could be a little one, or it could be huge. God listens to all sizes.

This is the perfect day to unload. Admit what you did and experience the forgiveness of God.

If we confess our sins, he is faithful and just and will forgive us our sins and purify us from all unrighteousness.

1 John 1:9

Think It Over

1. Have you ever confessed something to God?
2. Did you allow the feeling of guilt to lift?
3. Is there something you want to leave with God now?

Cocaine in the Bathtub

They must have been bright people. Most of us wouldn't have any idea how to carry this off.

A group of drug smugglers figured out how to "bond" cocaine into bathtubs, luggage pieces, and other objects. They would then ship the items into a country past the watchful eyes of the customs officers.

Once the objects were safely into their hands, they then had the ability to extract the drugs from the briefcases, suitcases, or bathroom fixtures.

Authorities explain that this was no simple project. The smugglers didn't merely brush the cocaine off and carry it away. They had to use laboratory processes to remove the drugs.

Previously, smugglers had put cocaine into bottles and moved them past customs. Innocent-looking perfume and shampoo were laced with drugs, which were later removed.

What kind of mind goes to work to devise evil schemes? Whoever concocted these processes had to be bright and intelligent. Why didn't they turn those capable brains to finding a cure for cancer or helping handicapped children or building a better water system?

Most of us have sharp minds. We don't have to be geniuses to think well. Some of the most amazing discoveries and inventions were made by men or women with quite ordinary mental capabilities.

Unfortunately, thousands, if not millions, of perfectly good minds dedicate themselves to evil causes. Too few of us use our considerable brainpower to serve the Lord.

Christian minds could:

Help feed the starving.
Write worshipful, uplifting music.
Find a cure for AIDS.
Communicate the Gospel.
Rescue children.
Reduce war.
Program computers.

Never limit what God can do with a brain that is dedicated to him. The Holy Spirit can lead you into fields and adventures that you cannot yet imagine. Ask God to open you up to the possibilities he might have waiting for your active mind.

Wouldn't it be a waste to smuggle cocaine when we could be serving Jesus Christ?

The mind of sinful man is death, but the mind controlled by the Spirit is life and peace.

Romans 8:6

Think It Over

1. Do you put your brainpower to work? little? some? much?
2. How would you like to serve God with your brain?
3. Ask God to accept your mind as a living sacrifice to him.

I Want What I Want

When a baby doesn't get what it wants, the baby cries, screams, and kicks until somebody makes it happy.

If a child fails to get what it wants, the child might hold its breath, stomp its feet, or kick a ball.

When an older child is told "No, not now," the older child might sulk, pout, complain, and even nag.

What happens if an adult doesn't get what he or she wants? Hopefully adults will:

- wait
- plan
- prepare
- be patient
- understand
- work

Not every adult does this. Some act like children. They might even behave like babies.

Suppose a teenager wants something. He thinks he has to have a CD player, a fourth pair of athletic shoes, a ski trip, a school jacket, or whatever. How do teens behave when they simply gotta have it?

The rap on teens is that they aren't good at waiting. Young people are into instant gratification. Delayed gratification is considered a bummer because they live "now."

If a teen wants something, is he or she likely to act like a baby or a child? Or will he act the way an adult is supposed to? Do teens throw fits, stomp out of rooms, yell and scream, or otherwise make a scene when they can't have what they want?

It's a hard choice. Teenagers are no longer children, yet they're not full-grown adults. When you want something — really bad — do you slide back into childhood, or do you move forward to adult behavior?

Adult behavior is marked by patience. Kids can't wait, but grown-ups can. The older we get, the wiser we get, and the more patient we become.

> A man's wisdom gives him patience.
> *Proverbs 19:11*

Think It Over

1. Are you a person who wants instant gratification?
2. Is your patience growing?
3. Do you want God to help you learn patience?

The Power of Lust

Normally when we think of lust, our thoughts turn to sex. We assume we're talking about well-proportioned bodies, nudity, cravings, and all that. Often that is exactly what we are discussing.

But it's a mistake to limit lust to the subject of sex. Most of us have a list of things we lust over. We might lust for:

- money
- power
- popularity
- athletic ability
- awards
- recognition
- cars
- jobs

The word lust simply means strong desire. Frankly, there isn't anything wrong with strong desires. A strong desire to help others, for example, is good.

Lust becomes an ugly word when it causes us to do things that are wrong. If we desire to make money, that can be good. But if we are greedy and would do anything to get money, that's bad.

If you desire sex, that's good. If your desire for sex causes you to do something immoral, that's bad.

If you desire a job, that's good. If you hurt others to get the job, that's bad.

If you desire friends, that's good. If you throw away your faith to get friends, that's bad.

The difference between desire and lust is often a question of:

How much you want it.
What you will do to get it.
Whom you will hurt to get it.
Whether you want the wrong thing.
How you will use it.

Smart people check out their desires with God. They want their "drives" to be in tune with what Christ wants.

For everything in the world—the cravings of sinful man, the lust of his eyes and the boasting of what he has and does—comes not from the Father but from the world. The world and its desires pass away, but the man who does the will of God lives forever.

1 John 2:16–17

Think It Over

1. Can you tell if your desires are getting out of hand? How?
2. Can you think of a time when you wanted something too much?
3. It makes sense to check out our desires with the heavenly Father.

Curfews and Boundaries

Even the oceans have boundaries. If they didn't, the entire world would be overrun with water, and life would be almost unbearable.

If there were no boundaries:

- rhinos would fly
- oatmeal wouldn't stay in the pan
- good teeth would keep falling out
- stereos couldn't be turned off
- buttons would keep popping open

Boundaries are limits, and limits are good. Curfews are simply limits that are placed on people so that:

- nights won't spill over into mornings
- waking hours won't invade sleeping hours
- parties won't run too long
- pleasant people won't lap over and become grouches
- idleness won't go too far
- decent behavior won't jump out of its banks

Surveys indicate that most teens have curfews. Probably most surveys would also suggest that teenagers hate curfews. A few teens have no set time to be home, and all of the other teens mention that to their parents at least once a week.

Not all of us hate boundaries. We go home, go to bed, get up, and try to avoid trouble. The problem is that too many young people don't know when to quit and go home. While they are learning their limitations, someone else has to set their boundaries.

Boundaries can sometimes be too strict. It can happen. But sensible, non-screaming, non-angry teenagers need to sit and talk to parents if the curfew isn't reasonable.

A teenager from South Carolina told me that he sat down with his parents and told them they still treated him like a fifth grader. He was reasonable and specific. After he explained the facts, they set limits more appropriate to his age. The problem is that teens too often ask for unrealistic changes.

Never curse the people who try to set reasonable boundaries. Everyone and everything must have a boundary. Otherwise, rain would fall inside the house.

Referring to water, the Bible says,

You set a boundary they cannot cross; never again will they cover the earth.

Psalm 104:9

Think It Over

1. What is your curfew?
2. Is it reasonable?
3. Have you ever thanked God for a curfew?

Evil Eats Us Up

Evil is real!

Anyone who reads the newspapers, watches television, or goes to school has to admit that evil exists. The world is filled with terrible, horrible, despicable acts. People are raped, tortured, mutilated, kidnapped, enslaved, murdered, and abused.

These are evil actions. They aren't lapses because someone had a bad hair day or the elastic gave out on their socks. They aren't misunderstandings or acts of rude behavior. They are wrong, harmful, painful ways to behave.

Evil is real! If evil has the opportunity, it will eat us up. People who aren't careful to resist evil could find themselves followers of that evil.

Have you ever

- lied about someone?
- stolen from a friend?
- cheated when giving change?
- picked on someone from another race?
- hit a person who couldn't fight back?

These are acts of evil. We don't have to murder or invade a country to behave in an evil way. All of us have the potential. And sometimes all of us can feel ourselves being drawn toward it.

Innocent, nice people who live in quiet, safe communities are often tempted to do totally despicable things. If conditions are right, each of us is capable of unspeakable acts.

We don't have to live in daily fear that we will do something mean. Instead, we need to draw closer to God and concentrate on doing his will. Living in harmony with our heavenly Father is the best protection we can get.

As a result, he does not live the rest of his earthly life for evil human desires, but rather for the will of God.

1 Peter 4:2

Think It Over

1. Have you ever wanted to really hurt someone?
2. Was the feeling scary?
3. Do you usually live closer to God or closer to evil?

When You Get the Uglies

"I never had a date when I was in high school." A pretty movie star shocked everyone when she admitted this.

"They used to call me bones. I wore big clothes so nobody would know what a rail I was," explained a successful model.

"I remember sitting home alone and depressed wondering why nobody liked me," said a television star.

"In high school I was a hall monitor and at ball games I worked the concession stands. Everybody agreed I was a geek," a sports commentator confessed.

Almost all of us get the uglies sometimes. Even the people who we think are always cool and confident feel like slime once in a while.

Nearly everyone fights the

- zit wars
- freak battles
- awkward angst
- hair horrors
- big ears fears
- chunky chills
- too short shakes

We worry about our looks. That's understandable. We go through adjustments, and we wonder what the final product will look like.

That's good. Spend some time improving your appearance. Just don't become obsessed by it. To hate your looks every day is to become obsessed.

Invest more time tuning up your inside. It would be a waste to bake a cake and spend all your efforts on the frosting. A good cake has fresh ingredients under the frosting.

Jesus put it this way. Don't use all of your energy washing the outside of a cup. The inside is what really needs to be clean.

Talking to God. Listening to God. Submitting to God. These are the things that give us lasting beauty.

> Blind Pharisee! First clean the inside of the cup and dish, and then the outside also will be clean.
>
> *Matthew 23:26*

Think It Over

1. How much time do you spend each day working on your outside appearance?
2. How much time do you spend cleaning the inside?
3. Can you think of an inner "blemish" or weakness that you would like God to help you with?

A Good Attitude

Look at the people who get into trouble—not the ones who are occasionally late with their homework or the teen who brought a lizard to school. Check out the ones who continuously do battle with teachers and administrators, those who act like they are at war with the vice principal.

Most teenagers who are in repeated trouble are the ones who have flunked attitude.

They hate authority.
They carry a chip on their shoulder.
They don't think anyone should tell them what to do.
They think they can try anything and probably should.
They believe they can't get caught and are particularly angry at the person who does catch them.
While not opposed to rules, they don't think rules should apply to them.
They don't consider themselves bad people and can't imagine why people get upset with them.
They insist that no one *ever* listens to them.

Many people who show crummy behavior flunked attitude first of all. Once we get an attitude, it's hard for us or anyone else to change our behavior.

Punishment is designed to alter behavior. Getting grounded, being sent to detention, or being thrown into jail are acts of power aimed at controlling our behavior, but the real goal is to change our attitude.

There are two good ways to change an attitude.

First, we can change it ourselves. If we are at war with life, we need to call a truce and make peace with our surroundings. If we don't, we will get hurt and hurt others.

Second, we can ask God to work through his Holy Spirit to give us a new attitude. God responds to that kind of invitation and helps us look at life in a new way.

Honestly I have seen it happen both ways. Some people get fed up with themselves and turn over a new leaf. Others call on spiritual resources and ask Christ to work in their lives. An attitude is a terrible tiger to tame, and often God's Spirit is the only hope we have.

Occasionally we need to give ourselves an attitude check. Christ is capable of altering our outlook on life and our reaction to it.

To be made new in the attitude of your minds; and to put on the new self, created to be like God in true righteousness and holiness.

Ephesians 4:23–24

Think It Over

1. In a seven-day week how many days do you have a good attitude?
2. What seems to affect your attitude for good or bad?
3. In which areas would you like to see God help you improve your attitude?

What's Your Nickname?

Have you ever looked at some of the nicknames given to baseball players? These are just a few.

Boog	Scooter	Lefty
Stump	Dizzy	Babe
Daffy	Sparky	Bucky
Catfish	The Train	The Mouth
Wahoo	The Bird	The Mick
The Georgia Peach	The Man	

Do you wonder how people pick up their nicknames? Some get them as children, others because of some habit they used to have. Often people are called a name long after anyone remembers why.

People are called "Skinny" when they are no longer thin. Some are called "Curly" even though they are bald. Others are called "Bud" because they don't like their real name.

There is a person in the Bible who has an interesting nickname. He was called "The Son of Encouragement." His real name was Joseph, but the Apostles called him Barnabas, which means "The Son of Encouragement."

How did Joseph get this name? Was his entire family a group of optimists who liked to make everyone feel perky? Did they run around saying uplifting things to everybody?

Suppose your friends were to give you a nickname. What might it be?

The Grump	The Christian	The Bright One
The Helper	The Goof	The Dork
The Cheerful One	The Lazy	The Pest
The Happy	The Gossip	The Good Friend

What nickname would you choose if you had to choose? Would we like to change our personality or attitude or behavior to the kind of nickname we would really like?

Joseph, a Levite from Cyprus, whom the apostles called Barnabas (which means Son of Encouragement).

Acts 4:36

Think It Over

1. Give yourself a nickname that would match your personality.
2. What would you like to change your nickname to?
3. What nickname do you think God would give you?